Defeat of the Spanish Armada

Books in the Battles Series:

✠ Battles of the Middle Ages ✠

Defeat of the Spanish Armada

by William W. Lace

ALLSTON BRANCH LIBRARY

Lucent Books, P.O. Box 289011, San Diego, CA 92198-9011

Library of Congress Cataloging-in-Publication Data

Lace, William W.
  Defeat of the Spanish Armada / by William W. Lace.
    p. cm. — (Battles of the Middle Ages)
  Includes bibliographical references and index.
  Summary: Examines the pivotal naval battle in which the upstart
  British defeated the supposedly invincible Spanish fleet, changing
  the balance of power in sixteenth century Europe.
  ISBN 1-56006-458-7 (alk. paper)
  1. Armada, 1588—Juvenile literature. 2. Great Britain—History,
Naval—Tudors, 1485–1603—Juvenile literature. 3. Spain—History,
Naval—16th century—Juvenile literature. [1. Armada, 1588. 2. Great
Britain—History, Naval—Tudors, 1485–1603. 3. Spain—History,
Naval—16th century.] I. Title. II. Series.
DA360.L26   1997
942.05'5—dc20   96-21508
                                                          CIP
                                                          AC

Contents

Foreword

Almost everyone would agree with William Tecumseh Sherman that war "is all hell." Yet the history of war, and battles in particular, is so fraught with the full spectrum of human emotion and action that it becomes a microcosm of the human experience. Soldiers' lives are condensed and crystallized in a single battle. As Francis Miller explains in his *Photographic History of the Civil War* when describing the war wounded, "It is sudden, the transition from marching bravely at morning on two sound legs, grasping your rifle in two sturdy arms, to lying at nightfall under a tree with a member forever gone."

Decisions made on the battlefield can mean the lives of thousands. A general's pique or indigestion can result in the difference between life and death. Some historians speculate, for example, that Napoleon's fateful defeat at Waterloo was due to the beginnings of stomach cancer. His stomach pain may have been the reason that the normally decisive general was sluggish and reluctant to move his troops. And what kept George McClellan from winning battles during the Civil War? Some scholars and contemporaries believe that it was simple cowardice and fear. Others argue that he felt a gut-wrenching unwillingness to engage in the war of attrition that was characteristic of that particular conflict.

Battle decisions can be magnificently brilliant and horribly costly. At the Battle of Thaspus in 47 B.C., for example, Julius Caesar, facing a numerically superior army, shrewdly ordered his troops onto a narrow strip of land bordering the sea. Just as he expected, his enemy thought he had accidentally trapped himself and divided their forces to surround his troops. By dividing their army, his enemy had given Caesar the strategic edge he needed to defeat them. Other battle orders result in disaster, as in the case of the Battle at Balaklava during the Crimean War in 1854. A British general gave the order to attack a force of withdrawing enemy Russians. But confusion in relaying the order resulted in the 670 men of the Light Brigade's charging in the wrong direction into certain death by heavy enemy cannon fire. Battles are the stuff of history on the grandest scale—their outcomes often determine whether nations are enslaved or liberated.

Moments in battles illustrate the best and worst of human character. In the feeling of terror and the us-versus-them attitude that accompanies war, the enemy can be dehumanized and treated with a contempt that is considered repellent in times of peace. At Wounded Knee, the distrust and anticipation of violence that grew between the Native Americans and American soldiers led to the senseless killing of ninety men, women, and children. And who can forget My Lai, where the deaths of old men, women, and children at the hands of American soldiers shocked an America already disillusioned with the Vietnam War. The murder of six million Jews will remain burned into the human conscience forever as the measure of man's inhumanity to man. These horrors cannot be forgotten. And yet, under the terrible conditions of battle, one can find acts of bravery, kindness, and altruism. During the Battle of Midway, the members of Torpedo Squadron 8, flying in hopelessly antiquated planes and without the benefit of air protection from fighters, tried bravely to fulfill their mission—to destroy the *Kido Butai,* the Japanese Carrier Striking Force. Without air support, the squadron was immediately set upon by Japanese fighters. Nevertheless, each bomber tried valiantly to hit his target. Each failed. Every man but one died in the effort. But by keeping the Japanese fighters busy, the squadron bought time and delayed further Japanese fighter attacks. In the aftermath of the Battle of Isandhlwana in South Africa in 1879, a force of thousands of Zulu warriors trapped a contingent of British troops in a small trading post. After repeated bloody attacks in which many died on both sides, the Zulus, their final victory certain, granted the remaining British their lives as a gesture of respect for their bravery. During World War I, American troops were so touched by the fate of French war orphans that they took up a collection to help them. During the Civil War, soldiers of the North and South would briefly forget that they were enemies and share smokes and coffee across battle lines during the endless nights. These acts seem all the more dramatic, more uplifting, because they indicate that people can continue to behave with humanity when faced with inhumanity.

Lucent Books' Battles Series highlights the vast range of the human character revealed in the ordeal of war. Dramatic narrative describes in exciting and accurate detail the commanders, soldiers, weapons, strategies, and maneuvers involved in each battle. Each volume includes a comprehensive historical context, explaining what brought the parties to war, the events leading to the battle, what factors made the battle important, and the effects it had on the larger war and later events.

The Battles Series also includes a chronology of important dates that gives students an overview, at a glance, of each battle. Sidebars create a broader context by adding enlightening details on leaders, institutions, customs, warships, weapons, and armor mentioned in the narration. Every volume contains numerous maps that allow readers to better visualize troop movements and strategies. In addition, numerous primary and secondary source quotations drawn from both past historical witnesses and modern historians are included. These quotations demonstrate to readers how and where historians derive information about past events. Finally, the volumes in the Battles Series provide a launching point for further reading and research. Each book contains a bibliography designed for student research, as well as a second bibliography that includes the works the author consulted while compiling the book.

Above all, the Battles Series helps illustrate the words of Herodotus, the fifth-century B.C. Greek historian now known as the "father of history." In the opening lines of his great chronicle of the Greek and Persian Wars, the world's first battle book, he set for himself this goal: "To preserve the memory of the past by putting on record the astonishing achievements both of our own and of other peoples; and more particularly, to show how they came into conflict."

Chronology of Events

1510
King Henry VIII of England and Catherine of Aragon are married.

King Henry VIII ruled England from 1509 to 1547.

1533
Henry VIII breaks with Roman Catholic Church, forms Church of England; Henry and Anne Boleyn are married; Princess Elizabeth born (September 7).

1547
Henry VIII dies; Edward VI becomes king of England.

1548
Netherlands unified under Emperor Charles V.

1553
Edward VI dies; Mary I becomes queen of England.

1554
Mary I and Philip II of Spain are married.

1555–1556
Philip II becomes king of the Netherlands and Spain.

1558
Calais, last English possession on the European continent, falls to France; Mary I dies; Elizabeth I becomes queen of England.

1562
First voyage of John Hawkins to Spanish America.

1566
Rebellion against Spain begins in the Netherlands; Philip sends duke of Alva to the Netherlands with large army.

1568
English ships destroyed at San Juan de Ulúa by Spaniards; Mary, Queen of Scots, imprisoned in England.

1570
Elizabeth is excommunicated by Roman Catholic Church.

1577
Prince William of Orange conquers most of southern Netherlands.

1578
Duke of Parma sent to reconquer Netherlands for Spain.

1580
Philip II adds Portugal to his empire.

1584
William of Orange is assassinated.

1585
Spanish agents bring about civil war in France.

May 19   Philip orders seizure of English ships and goods in Spanish ports.

October   Sir Francis Drake attacks cities in Spain and Spanish America.

October 24   Philip asks pope to bless and help pay for an invasion of England.

December   Philip writes to Santa Cruz and Parma asking for suggestions for invasion of England.

1586

July 26 Philip sends plans for invasion to Santa Cruz and Parma.

September Mary, Queen of Scots, implicated in Babington Plot against Elizabeth.

1587

February 12 Mary, Queen of Scots, executed, wills her claim to English throne to Philip.

April 29 Drake raids Cádiz.

May 31 Drake leaves Spain.

September 14 Philip changes invasion plans, which now call for Armada to meet Parma's army.

September 25 Santa Cruz returns with Spanish fleet, having escorted treasure ships from America.

1588

February 9 Santa Cruz dies in Lisbon.

February 11 Philip appoints duke of Medina Sidonia to lead Armada.

April 25 Armada dedicated at Lisbon cathedral service.

May 28 Armada sails from Lisbon.

June 3 Lord Howard joins Drake in Plymouth with most of English fleet.

June 19 Armada, running short of supplies, arrives at Corunna.

July 17 English fleet leaves Plymouth for Corunna.

July 21 Armada leaves Corunna bound for English Channel.

July 29 Armada arrives within sight of England; English fleet leaves Plymouth.

July 30 English fleet sails around Armada to gain "weather gauge."

July 31 First battle fought off Plymouth; Armada loses *Rosario* and *San Salvador*.

August 2 Battle fought off Portland Bill.

August 3 Howard divides English fleet into squadrons.

August 4 Battle fought off Isle of Wight.

August 6 Armada arrives at Calais.

August 8 Howard sends fire ships to scatter Armada; Battle of Gravelines is fought.

August 9 Armada is saved from destruction by shift in wind, sails into North Sea with English in pursuit.

August 12 Howard ends pursuit, orders English fleet to turn south.

Spanish sailors flee the approaching English fire ships.

August 18 Howard's fleet arrives in England; Elizabeth speaks to army at Tilbury.

August 21 Armada sails west from North Sea into Atlantic Ocean.

August 22 Storms begin to scatter Armada.

August–September Dozens of Armada's ships wrecked on Irish coast.

September 21 Medina Sidonia arrives in Spain with remnant of Armada.

November 24 Service of thanksgiving held by English at St. Paul's Cathedral.

Making History, Changing Warfare

For more than a thousand years, ships were used in battles on the sea. Here, the Spanish Armada battles enemy ships.

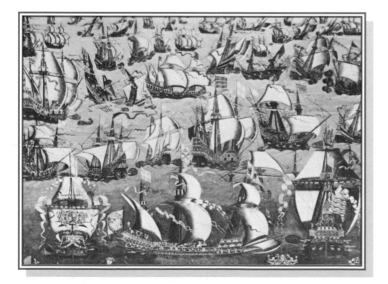

Some battles are famous because they change the course of history. Their outcomes alter the fate of nations and peoples, changing the face of politics, religion, economics, and society. Their effects echo through the centuries, long after the guns are silent and the smoke clears.

Other battles are famous because they signal dramatic changes in warfare. New and increasingly destructive weapons take center stage as humans devise ever more effective ways of slaughtering one another. New defenses are then developed to make the latest weapons obsolete. Military tactics employed for generations are swept away by a commander who invents a new strategy.

Rarely, however, is a battle considered a turning point both in world history and in warfare. Such a conflict occurred in the summer of 1588 when Spain, ruler of all that was known of America as well as most of Europe, set out to invade England. To carry his soldiers to the stubborn little island, King Philip II of Spain amassed the greatest fleet of ships the world had known—the Spanish Armada. Since England had practically no land defenses, all that stood in Spain's way was the smaller English navy.

When the two fleets met in battle, naval warfare changed forever. For more than a thousand years since the days of the ancient Greeks and Romans, European sea battles had been fought in the Mediterranean Sea between fleets of galleys rowed by slaves or prisoners. Victory was won by ramming an opponent or pulling alongside and sending soldiers swarming onto the enemy deck. Now, for the first time, two large fleets of sailing ships would collide. The tactics employed and the lessons learned would govern war at sea until the advent of the aircraft carrier during World War II.

What Was at Stake

While the Europeans of 1588 could not have known of the battle's military significance, they nevertheless realized just how much was at stake. If England fell, Spain would be the unchallenged master of Europe. Not only would this have great economic and political consequences, but it also would reaffirm the domination of the Roman Catholic Church and threaten the Protestant religion with extinction.

Even the stars predicted that the year 1588 would bring enormous change and upheaval. Most people of the time believed in astrology—that the future could be predicted by the movement of the stars. In the 1400s, a German astrologer known as Regiomontanus forecast a year of terror and doom and put his prediction into verse, widely quoted as the fateful year dawned:

> When after Christ's birth there be expired
> Of hundreds, fifteen year, eighty and eight,
> There comes the time of dangers to be feared
> And all mankind with dolors [woes] it shall fright.
> For if the world in that year do not fall,
> If sea and land then perish nor decay,
> Yet Empires all, and Kingdoms alter shall,
> And man to ease himself shall have no way.

What empires and kingdoms were to be altered, which men would be uneasy, Regiomontanus did not say.

CHAPTER ONE

Drifting Toward War

S pain and England, bitter enemies when the Armada sailed in 1588, had been allies when the century opened. At that time, France was England's traditional rival, as it had been for more than two hundred years. As the balance of power in Europe shifted, however, the twin forces of economics and religion drove a wedge between England and Spain and brought them to war.

France was the mightiest nation in Europe in 1500. England, under King Henry VII, was still recovering from thirty years of civil war. Spain had only recently been united under King Ferdinand II of Aragon and his queen, Isabella of Castile.

It was natural that England and Spain should form an alliance against France, and in 1501 a marriage was arranged between Henry's oldest son, Arthur, and Catherine of Aragon, daughter of Ferdinand and Isabella.

When Arthur died the next year, Henry did not want to give up either the alliance with Spain or Catherine's dowry—an amount of money paid by a bride's family to the groom. So, instead of returning Catherine and the dowry to Spain, he arranged for her to be engaged to his second son, also named Henry, who was twelve

Catherine of Aragon (above) married Henry VIII (right) in 1510. When Catherine failed to produce a male heir, Henry sought to annul the marriage.

years old at the time. Until Henry was an adult and the wedding could take place, Catherine was kept in England on a meager allowance.

Henry VIII became king when his father died in 1509 and married Catherine the next year. At first, the marriage was a happy one, with Catherine a loving and helpful queen. As the years went by, however, she failed to give Henry the male heir he desperately wanted. Numerous pregnancies resulted in only one child, a sickly daughter named Mary.

Meanwhile, Henry fell in love with one of Catherine's ladies-in-waiting, Anne Boleyn. About 1530, after Anne refused to become Henry's mistress and insisted on marriage, Henry set out to obtain an annulment, or cancellation, of his marriage with Catherine. Catherine refused to be put aside quietly. She appealed to the pope, head of the Roman Catholic Church and the only person who could grant such an annulment. At this point, Henry's love life became the center of an international political struggle.

When Anne Boleyn, mistress of Henry VIII, demanded that he annul his marriage to Catherine, she caused an international controversy.

Royal Marriages

Spain had used royal marriages to form alliances with countries other than England. Catherine's sister, Juana, had married Philip the Handsome, heir of Maximilian I, ruler of the Holy Roman Empire, a huge confederation that included most of present-day Austria, Hungary, Germany, Belgium, the Netherlands, and Italy. Philip succeeded his father as emperor but died in 1506, leaving his six-year-old son, Charles V, emperor. By the time he was nineteen, Charles had also inherited the throne of Spain, including the vast Spanish possessions in the Americas.

So it was that when Catherine of Aragon appealed to the pope to deny Henry VIII's request for an annulment, she also appealed for help to Charles, her nephew. This placed the pope in an awkward position. He did not want to anger the king of England, but he wanted even less to anger the more powerful Charles, who as ruler of much of Italy was in a position to force the pope to do his will. For his part, Charles was against the annulment, which not only would be an insult to his aunt, but which also would threaten to weaken the alliance between England and Spain.

The pope delayed a decision so long that the impatient Henry at last broke from the Roman Catholic Church in 1533, established the Church of England, got his annulment, and was able to marry Anne Boleyn, who by now had finally yielded to Henry and was pregnant. The new queen, however, had no more luck than the old one in producing a son. On September 7, 1533, another princess was born. She was named Elizabeth after Henry's mother.

Henry had formed a new church only to free himself of Catherine, not from any religious motives. He wanted to keep the church as it had always been, only without a pope. He had not wanted to make the English church Protestant, as those who broke away from Roman Catholicism were called. Church leaders in England, however, took matters far beyond what Henry intended. By the time he died in 1547, the country was firmly Protestant.

Henry had finally succeeded in having a son, Edward, by a third wife, Anne Boleyn having been executed for adultery. Edward VI was a frail child of ten when he came to the throne, but he was an ardent Protestant. During his reign, the Church of England began to be less and less like the Catholic Church and more like the more extreme Protestant churches of Europe. Laws were passed against the Catholic minority, and English Catholics had to worship in secret.

Bloody Mary

When Edward VI died of tuberculosis in 1553, the throne went to his oldest sister, Mary. Mary was as extreme a Catholic as Edward had been a Protestant. She was determined to do two things: to make England a Catholic country once more and to restore ties between England and her native Spain. To help accomplish both goals, she offered herself in marriage to Philip of Spain, son of Emperor Charles V. They were married on July 25, 1554.

Philip was then twenty-seven years old and had ruled Spain in his father's name since he was sixteen. While he could be as charming and dashing as any young nobleman, he was serious and deliberate by nature, unlike his extravagant father. Philip had already been married, but his wife, Maria of Portugal, had died giving birth to a son, Carlos. He wed Mary of England, eleven years older, only out of a sense of duty to his father. Mary, however, fell passionately in love with her younger husband. She pledged English troops to help fight Spain's wars against France.

The marriage was highly unpopular with the English people. They did not want to be ruled by a Spaniard and to be dragged into Spain's wars. This ill feeling reached its height when, in 1558, France captured the port city of Calais, the last English possession on the European continent. The English blamed the loss of Calais on Mary, who had sent English troops to fight alongside the Spaniards against the French instead of keeping them at home to face the threat to her own country.

Whether England was to be Catholic or Protestant greatly concerned rulers Edward VI (left) and Mary Tudor (below, with Philip II). Edward wanted the country to be Protestant, while Mary wanted it returned to Catholicism and married Philip of Spain to help achieve her goal.

The Prudent King

While many of the European kings and queens of his time were head-strong, dashing, and lavish, King Philip II of Spain was the complete opposite—slow, careful, plain in life and dress, and a person who paid attention to the smallest details. One historian called him the Prudent King. Another called him "the chief clerk of the Spanish Empire."

He preferred to work alone at his desk, sometimes as long as fourteen hours a day, examining documents and issuing written instructions. He avoided face-to-face meetings whenever possible. Once, when a general asked for an audience to explain plans for a war, Philip wrote, "If you happen to be close to court, it might be useful to hear the details from you in person, but . . . I think it would be best if you wrote."

While Queen Elizabeth I of England was famous for her sharp temper, Philip was known for his patience. Once, after Philip finished writing a long letter, a nervous clerk, intending to sprinkle sand over the paper to dry it, picked up the wrong container and poured ink instead. Instead of ordering the fellow punished, the king calmly pointed to the two containers and said, "No, *that* is the ink. *This* is the sand."

Philip's devotion to religion stood out even in an age when most people were very devout. He considered the Armada a holy enterprise and in his written orders devoted as much space to how the crews should conduct themselves as to the actual military plans. He told his admirals, for instance, that there was to be no swearing or blaspheming aboard ships, a very optimistic order, indeed, given the normal conduct of sailors.

Even Philip's hobbies revolved around religion. He collected religious books and art but was most known for having Europe's largest collection of relics—bits and pieces of saints' bodies—which were supposed to have great powers. At one point, his collection included 7,422 items, among which were 12 entire bodies, 144 heads, and 306 complete arms or legs. "We only know of three saints of whom we do not have some part or other here," the monk in charge of Philip's relics once bragged.

Although he ruled the world's mightiest empire wisely and well, he was basically a humble man who considered himself unfit for the job. He once wrote:

> I know very well that I should be at some other station in life, one not as exalted as the one God has given me, which for me alone is terrible. And many criticize me for this. Please God that in heaven we shall be better treated.

Philip II's devotion to religion drove him to collect over seven thousand holy relics.

Even more unpopular was Mary's zeal in trying to return England to the Catholic Church. Late in 1554, Catholicism was formally made the country's official religion, and those who refused to give up Protestant worship faced heavy fines or even death. More than three hundred Protestants were burned at the stake for defending their beliefs during Mary's reign. Because of this, she has been known throughout history as Bloody Mary.

Much of the objection to the restoration of the Catholic Church was economic. In 1535, Henry VIII had seized all church property in England. Many rich monasteries and the lands surrounding them were distributed by the king to his nobles. Naturally, these nobles were bitterly opposed when Mary announced her intention to restore all the church's property.

Philip stayed in England only slightly more than a year. In 1555, his father, worn out by decades of trying to keep order in his vast empire, decided to give up his throne. He gave his central European possessions to his brother Ferdinand, and Philip received the rest. Philip, now King Philip II, left England in September and was to return only for short visits.

Although Elizabeth I (pictured) returned the Church of England to Protestantism, she allowed Catholics to practice privately in their homes.

Elizabeth Becomes Queen

Mary wanted desperately to have a child. Only then could she be confident that her religious program for England would continue. If she died childless, her younger half-sister, Elizabeth, would rule. Although Elizabeth had been outwardly a Catholic, Mary suspected she was a Protestant at heart. Mary's prayers were not answered. Several times she announced she was pregnant, but these were either psychosomatic (mentally induced false pregnancies) or symptoms of the cancer that finally killed her on November 17, 1558, making twenty-five-year-old Elizabeth queen of England.

When Elizabeth I was crowned, the two main questions in the minds of her subjects were, first, whom would she marry and, second, what would she do about religion. She kept everyone guessing the answer to the first question for decades, flirting with one suitor after another and, in the end, never marrying at all.

The second question could not be avoided. England had been pulled back and forth between Protestantism and Catholicism for a generation. The people wanted peace and an end to persecution. The duke of Norfolk advised Elizabeth, "Let your Highness assure yourself that England can bear no more changes in religion. It hath been bowed so oft that if it should be bent again it would break."

In the end, she made a decision in keeping with her own feelings and those of her subjects. The Church of England was reestablished, and everyone was required to attend its services. Catholic worship was tolerated only if it was done in the privacy of one's home. Elizabeth could never have been at home in the church that had branded her a bastard, claiming that Henry VIII's annulment was illegal. Also, the highly independent Elizabeth did not want to yield any authority to the pope in Rome. As for her people, Mary's religious persecutions had aroused such hatred that Elizabeth probably could not have kept the country Catholic even if she wanted to.

A Marriage Proposal

Despite Elizabeth's return to Protestantism, King Philip did not turn against his former sister-in-law. Indeed, in 1559 he offered to become her husband. Although he wrote that he proposed marriage "only to serve God and to stop that lady making the changes in religion," it is possible that while in England, he had been attracted to the lively, witty Elizabeth, especially compared to her dour, dowdy half-sister.

Elizabeth refused Philip's offer—her first of many refusals—but let him down gently, claiming to be unworthy of such an honor. She wrote to him that she nevertheless wanted to keep his friendship. That much, at least, was true. Elizabeth had almost no army and almost no money as a result of the French wars. She could not afford to have the powerful Philip as an enemy. The friendship lasted about ten years. In the end, however, it was pulled apart by two separate developments.

In the late 1400s, Spain and Portugal were the only European countries trading in the New World and in Asia. To prevent conflict, in 1493 the pope proclaimed the Treaty of Tordesillas, which gave Spain rights to most of the Americas, the Caribbean islands, and the western Pacific. Portugal got Brazil, the coast of Africa, India, and the eastern Pacific.

Despite being left out of the agreement, England began establishing trade routes between Africa and the Americas in the 1550s. The first voyage of Elizabeth's reign was by John Hawkins in 1562, who bought or captured slaves in Africa then sold them to Spanish settlements in the Caribbean at a huge profit. Even the queen began to invest in this enterprise.

At first, Philip merely tolerated this violation of his monopoly but at last he decided to put a stop to it. In 1568, Hawkins's

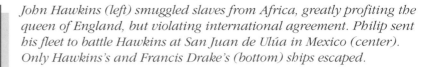

John Hawkins (left) smuggled slaves from Africa, greatly profiting the queen of England, but violating international agreement. Philip sent his fleet to battle Hawkins at San Juan de Ulúa in Mexico (center). Only Hawkins's and Francis Drake's (bottom) ships escaped.

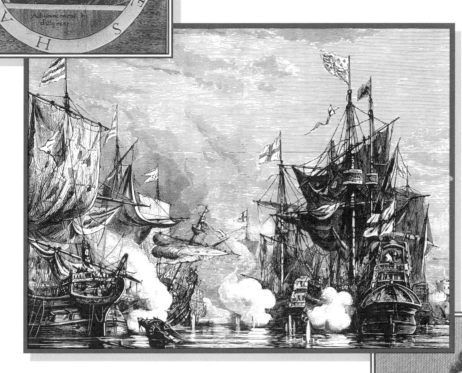

ships were at San Juan de Ulúa in Mexico when a Spanish fleet appeared at the mouth of the Mexican harbor. The Spanish commander had signaled that the English would be allowed to leave safely but instead rushed and boarded the English ships. Only two ships escaped—the *Minion,* with Hawkins in command, and the *Judith,* commanded by one of Hawkins's best young captains, Francis Drake.

Undeclared War

The English were furious. Not only had their ships been taken by treachery, but some of the captured sailors were burned at the stake for their Protestant beliefs. Elizabeth wanted revenge and she wanted more profits from America, but she did not want war with Spain. She promised Philip

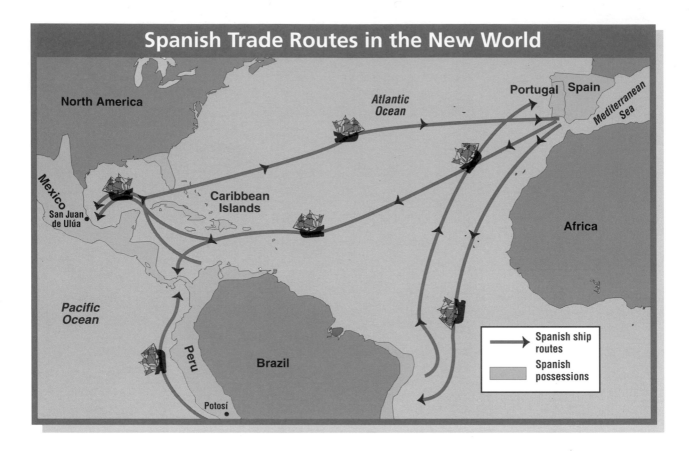

Spanish Trade Routes in the New World

that English adventures in America would stop, but she secretly encouraged them. The result was an undeclared war on Spain by English "sea dogs"—mainly Drake.

The second development was the revolt of the Netherlands against Spanish rule. Philip's father, Charles V, had unified the seventeen semi-independent counties of the Netherlands earlier in the century. In 1548, they were placed for the first time under a single administrative structure.

The Netherlands prospered under Spanish rule as never before. Since the voyages of Christopher Columbus, the center of trade activity had shifted from the Mediterranean Sea to the Atlantic Ocean. The Netherlands were in the perfect location to take advantage of this change. Goods from all over the world came to Dutch ports to be shipped inland on several great rivers. Traders from Spain, England, France, Germany, and Scandinavia found the Netherlands to be a central location, and it quickly became the commercial and financial capital of the Spanish empire.

The Dutch burghers, or wealthy businessmen, soon began to grow restless under Spanish rule. For centuries, they had been free to do pretty much as they pleased. They did not object to making higher profits, but it stung them to see much of the wealth they created going to Spain.

The Dutch also resented Spain's attempt to impose a rigid Catholicism on the country. Although many of the Dutch were Catholics, the various Protestant churches such as the Lutherans and the Calvinists had many followers. In an attempt to strengthen the Catholic Church, Philip created several new Catholic bishops in the Netherlands, passed new laws against Protestantism, and decided to bring the Inquisition—a religious court that had the power to execute those who refused to accept the Catholic Church—to the Netherlands.

Cities in the Netherlands such as Amsterdam (above) profited from Spain's takeover. The Dutch resented Spain's intolerance toward Protestantism and its trials of heretics, called the Inquisition (below).

The Dutch Rebellion

In the minds of the Dutch, both economic and religious domination by Spain were combined into a single grievance. They expressed this discontent through religion. In 1566, Dutch Protestants began holding open-air prayer meetings with armed men standing guard against any interference by Spanish officials. Soon the Dutch began breaking into Catholic churches, smashing altars and statues of saints. Philip responded by ordering ten thousand Spanish troops under his most experienced commander, the duke of Alva, to go to the Netherlands and put down the revolt.

The decision to send Alva to the Netherlands dramatically altered the balance of power in northern Europe. France, England, and the independent states of Germany found Philip's action unacceptable because this large army permanently based in the Netherlands could be easily used against any of them. All now offered support, either troops or arms, to William of Nassau, prince of Orange, who had given up a life of wealth and ease to lead his Dutch countrymen against the might of Spain.

Slowly, the rebels began to succeed. Much of Spain's military might was useless in the Netherlands, where broad rivers, wide marshes, and a system of canals made troop movements a nightmare. An English traveler of the time wrote that two of the largest provinces, Holland and Zeeland, were "the great bog of Europe . . . a universal quagmire." Furthermore, Alva could not be supplied by sea. Dutch "sea beggars" in their small, swift cromsters patrolled the shallow waters along the coast, blockading the

When Spain sent troops to the Netherlands (below, right) to crack down on widespread rebellion, France, England, and Germany offered to send troops to aid William of Nassau, prince of Orange (pictured), in his fight against the Spanish.

ports and preventing the Spanish from landing additional troops. When the Spanish tried to force their way on shore in 1572, their fleet ran aground and was wrecked.

Alva was recalled to Spain in disgrace in 1573. In 1575, with the cost of the rebellion draining his treasury, Philip cut off payment to his troops in the Netherlands, most of whom mutinied or deserted. By May of 1577, William of Orange was master of all the southern provinces.

Spain's fleet is stopped from resupplying its armies in the Netherlands by patrolling sea beggars.

A Controversial Queen

Relations between England and Spain had continued to worsen. As long as Queen Elizabeth remained childless, her cousin Mary, Queen of Scots, was next in line for the throne. Although queen of Scotland, which was staunchly Protestant, Mary had been reared in the French court and was a devout Catholic. In 1568, she and her lover brought about the murder of her husband. The outraged Scots rose in rebellion, and Mary took refuge in England.

Elizabeth was in a predicament. If she returned Mary to Scotland, she might be sending her to her death at the hands of her subjects, something Elizabeth, as a fellow ruler, found unthinkable. On the other hand, if she gave Mary her freedom, she feared Mary would try to stir the Catholics in England to rebel. In the end Elizabeth did

The Virgin Queen

Elizabeth I of England was like her adversary Philip II of Spain, in many ways. Both were extremely cautious and deliberate. Indeed, it was Elizabeth's practice to put off decisions as long as she possibly could. "I have let time pass," she once wrote to the king of France, "which I generally find helps more than reasoning."

Like Philip, she was a very private person. She had learned growing up that keeping one's thoughts to oneself might mean keeping one's head. Even though she refused to be drawn into plots against her sister, Mary I, she almost was executed for treason.

Outwardly, Elizabeth was everything Philip was not. She loved the gaiety of the court, with its games, tournaments, hunting, feasts, and dancing almost every night. Hers was a dazzling court, and she took pains to be most dazzling of all, covering herself with the most expensive clothes and jewels.

Although her ministers pleaded with her to marry so that she could have children to inherit the throne, she never took that step. She loved to flirt and had numerous suitors, including princes from throughout Europe, but probably knew all along she did not want a husband with whom she would have to share power. "God's death," she once shouted at the earl of Leicester, "I will have here but one mistress and no master."

Where Philip was placid and calm, Elizabeth was highly emotional and had a furious temper. She could curse as fluently as any soldier of her guard and was known to box the ears of some of her most noble ministers when they displeased her.

While she was extravagant where her own wardrobe and possessions were concerned, she was extraordinarily tightfisted when it came to running the government. She complained about the cost of everything, especially war. She never agreed to give her army or navy the supplies they needed. One of the blackest marks against her is her treatment after the Armada campaign of her sailors, many of whom wound up unpaid and begging in the streets.

Lavish in her personal spending, Elizabeth I resented spending money to run the government.

neither. Mary was treated with all honor and given the comforts of a queen, but she was housed in remote castles under the close watch of guardians thoroughly trusted by Elizabeth. She was permitted to go nowhere and to see no one without Elizabeth's permission. This confinement would last nineteen years.

Catholic Europe was enraged by the confinement, arguing that Mary was lawfully queen of Scotland and should be restored to her throne. The pope urged Philip to invade England and replace Elizabeth with Mary, but Philip, although furious at Elizabeth, was not willing to go this far. He feared that if Elizabeth were removed, Mary, Queen of Scots, would make England a French ally.

In 1570, the pope issued a proclamation freeing the English Catholics from any allegiance to Elizabeth and said that anyone who removed her from the throne by assassination would have the blessing of the church. The next year, the first of many such plots—undertaken with the cooperation of Mary and the Spanish ambassador to England—was discovered and thwarted. The break between Elizabeth and Philip was now complete.

Mary, Queen of Scots, tried to incite English Catholics to rebel.

Some of Elizabeth's ministers wanted her to go to war, but Elizabeth knew that England was far too weak. Besides, she hated the expense of war. She did not mind, however, if her sailors took revenge for her, preying on Spanish shipping in what amounted to an undeclared war. Between 1572 and 1577 England launched eleven expeditions against Spain's possessions in America and against treasure fleets bringing New World silver to Philip, who desperately needed all his revenue to pay his army in the Netherlands.

Philip felt that he had to end the Dutch rebellion before he could deal with England. In 1578, he sent his nephew Alessandro Farnese, duke of Parma, to the Netherlands. This brilliant general built up a large force known as the Army of Flanders and, by force and bribes, began to win back some of the territory lost to William of Orange.

Philip believed that brilliant general Alessandro Farnese (pictured) was capable of ending the rebellion in the Netherlands.

The Taking of Portugal

Philip soon was to grow more powerful than ever. Dom Sebastian, king of Portugal, was killed in 1578 and had no son to succeed him. Sebastian's mother was Philip's sister, giving Philip a claim to the Portuguese throne. Spanish land and sea forces overwhelmed Portugal and Philip was made king. With the addition of Portugal's overseas possessions, Philip now ruled the largest empire the world had ever known.

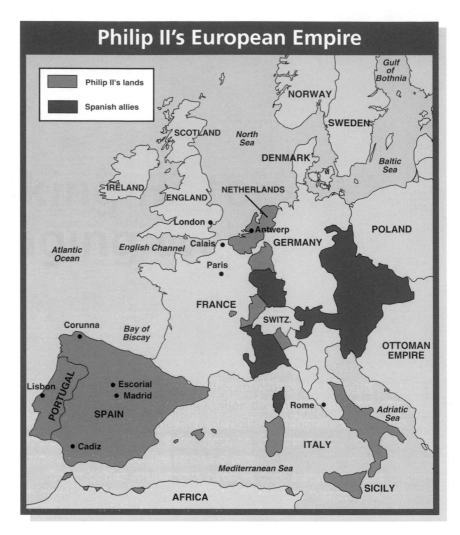

Philip II's European Empire

▨	Philip II's lands
▉	Spanish allies

NORWAY
SWEDEN
Gulf of Bothnia
SCOTLAND
North Sea
DENMARK
Baltic Sea
IRELAND
ENGLAND
NETHERLANDS
London
Antwerp
Calais
GERMANY
POLAND
Atlantic Ocean
English Channel
Paris
FRANCE
SWITZ.
OTTOMAN EMPIRE
Corunna
Bay of Biscay
PORTUGAL
Lisbon
Escorial
Madrid
Rome
Adriatic Sea
SPAIN
Cadiz
ITALY
Mediterranean Sea
SICILY
AFRICA

Philip now also had the world's most powerful navy. His leading admiral, Don Alvaro de Bazán, marquis of Santa Cruz, had captured twelve heavy galleons—heavily armed sailing ships—from Portugal. Adding these ships to the smaller warships Spain already had, Santa Cruz defeated the naval forces of Dom António, an illegitimate son of Sebastian who was trying to resist Philip's rule from his base in the Azores islands. The battle was fought at close range with Spanish ships using grapples—ropes with metal hooks—to pull enemy ships alongside so that soldiers could board them. When the naval battle was won, Santa Cruz landed soldiers on the main island of Terceira.

Spain's success in the Atlantic was followed by success in the Netherlands. Using military and diplomatic skill, Parma was well on his way to restoring Spanish rule. In the summer of 1584, his army captured the important towns of Bruges and Ghent and began to construct a blockade of the Scheldt River that would cut the principal Dutch city, Antwerp, from the sea. In July, the Dutch suffered another blow when William of Orange was murdered by one of Parma's agents.

Spanish troops attempt to battle anti-Spanish rebels in the Netherlands.

England's situation was grave. There seemed to be little to stop Spain from gaining full control of the Netherlands. Should that happen, one of Elizabeth's ministers wrote, Philip's power would be "so formidable to all the rest of Christendom as that Her Majesty shall no wise be able with her own power nor with the aid of any other, neither by sea nor land, to withstand his attempts." In 1585, to make matters worse, Spanish agents engineered a civil war in France that rendered that nation powerless to help the Dutch.

Still, Elizabeth hesitated, unwilling to declare war. Then, on May 19, 1585, Philip issued an order seizing all English ships and English goods in Spanish ports. He did this to frighten Elizabeth into stopping her ships from attacking those of Spain and to stop any thoughts of a formal alliance with the Dutch.

The Treaty of Nonsuch

Philip's action had exactly the opposite effect. On August 20, the Treaty of Nonsuch—named after one of Elizabeth's palaces—formally pledged England to provide more than seven thousand troops and £126,000 a year to the Dutch rebels. The English troops would be led by the queen's favorite courtier, Robert Dudley, earl of Leicester.

Instead of stopping raids on Spain's possessions, Elizabeth increased them. In the fall of 1585, an English fleet commanded by Francis Drake attacked the coastal towns of Vigo and Bayona in Spain itself, sacked the Spanish city of Santiago in the Cape Verde Islands, and then captured and burned the oldest Spanish city in the New World, Santo Domingo on the island of Hispaniola.

For Philip of Spain, this was the last straw. The Netherlands could wait. He would first deal with England and her queen, whom he had once offered to marry and who now caused him such grief.

El Draque

The most famous sailor of his day, and certainly the most feared by his enemies, was Sir Francis Drake. The name El Draque (the Dragon) struck such fear into Spanish captains who encountered him that they frequently surrendered without even a hint of a fight.

Drake was born sometime in the early 1540s, the son of a farmer in Tavistock, north of the seaport of Plymouth. His father, a passionate Protestant, was forced to leave his farm during the reign of Catholic queen Mary I and lived on an abandoned ship in the Medway River south of London, preaching his religion to sailors. Young Francis became as much a Protestant as his father and thus a lifelong and steadfast enemy of Spain.

Drake learned seamanship by working on small ships that carried cargoes along the English coast and in 1566 was given a place in the slave-trading expedition of John Hawkins, a cousin. He sailed again with Hawkins in 1567 and was given his first command, the *Judith*, in which he barely escaped the Spaniards at San Juan de Ulúa.

Drake's most famous voyage took place from 1577 to 1580 when he sailed through the Strait of Magellan at the southern tip of South America and raided the undefended Spanish settlements from Chile to California. When he returned in his ship, the *Golden Hind*, Queen Elizabeth I, who had invested in his expedition and earned a fabulous profit, came aboard and made Drake a knight. At the same time, she innocently told Spain's ambassador to England that she had no idea what Drake had been up to.

Drake was described by someone who knew him as "short, thick-set and very robust . . . of fine countenance [face] with a fair, reddish beard and a ruddy [red] complexion." He loved luxury and aboard his ships ate from golden plates while musicians played in the background. He treated his men well but expected complete obedience and was quick to punish those who disobeyed him. On his voyage around the world, one of his officers, Thomas Doughty, led a mutiny. Drake had him executed—after first entertaining him at a lavish dinner.

The victory over the Spanish Armada was the height of Drake's career. In 1589 he led an expedition against some remaining Armada ships at Lisbon that turned out to be a disaster. Drake returned to England in disgrace and settled in Plymouth, where he became mayor. In 1595 he came out of retirement to sail once more with Hawkins to the West Indies. This expedition, too, was a failure and one from which Drake never returned. He died of a fever off the coast of Panama and was buried at sea on January 28, 1596.

The activities of Drake and the other English sea dogs had injured not only Philip's reputation, but also his credit with major European bankers, who began to question his ability to maintain the flow of silver from the Americas. On October 24, 1585, Philip wrote to the pope. Asking the blessing of the church—and financial support—he agreed to prepare for the invasion of England.

CHAPTER TWO

The Enterprise of England

For years, King Philip II of Spain had been urged by the pope and others to invade England. The slow, precise king was in no hurry. He once said, "In so great an enterprise as that of England, it is fitting to move with feet of lead." In the autumn of 1585, though, deliberation turned to haste. Philip was determined to invade England, and the sooner the better. A combination of Spanish incompetence and English daring, however, would delay his dream for almost three years.

Unlike the lively and dazzling Elizabeth I of England, Philip lived almost like a monk in El Escorial, his combination

Philip II (pictured) and his residence El Escorial (left), where he lived a monklike existence.

A Crusade by Sea

From the very first, the principal purpose of the Armada in the mind of King Philip II of Spain was to restore the Catholic Church in England, or at least to ensure that English Catholics had freedom of worship. To be sure, the invasion had economic motives, namely to stop English raids on Spanish shipping from the Americas, but, as Medina Sidonia wrote in his orders to the Armada:

> The principal reason which has moved his Majesty to undertake this enterprise is his desire to serve God, and to convert to His Church many peoples and souls who are now oppressed by the heretical enemies of our holy Catholic faith, and are subjected to their sects and errors. In order that this aim should be kept constantly before the eyes of all I enjoin [urge] you to see that before embarking, all ranks [of men] be confessed [by priests] and absolved, with due contrition for their sins.

Furthermore, the duke wrote, his officers were to "take particular care in the Armada against sin of any kind, but especially the sin of blasphemy [cursing], by providing heavy penalties." Since sailors were known even then for their rough language, it is difficult to imagine that this order was fully carried out.

Before the Armada sailed from Lisbon, Medina Sidonia issued orders that all ships should be searched for women, who would be put ashore as an "evident inconvenience" and an offense to God. Nevertheless, some young officers may have smuggled sweethearts or mistresses aboard. In Norway, a report later was made that after an Armada ship wrecked on that coast, the bodies of several women with beautiful clothes and jewelry were washed ashore.

To see to the religious needs of the men of the Armada, 180 priests were taken along. Everyone was expected to attend at least one church service each week. Every morning at dawn, the ships' cabin boys gathered at the foot of the mainmast to sing "Salve Regina." At dusk they sang "Ave Maria."

monastery and palace high in the mountains above Madrid. Intensely religious, he lived in a small set of rooms from which he could see the church altar and hear the monks chanting mass. There, Philip conducted almost all of his empire's business, preferring to read reports and write instructions rather than deal with people face-to-face.

So it was that in December 1585 he wrote to the duke of Parma in the Netherlands and to Santa Cruz, who now carried the title of Captain General of the Ocean Sea. Both had suggested to the king in the past that he invade England. Now, he asked them to give him specific plans.

Santa Cruz proposed a greatly enlarged version of his campaign against the Portuguese in the Azores. His plan was a simple one: to amass a force so large as to be irresistible. He would need, he wrote to Philip in March 1586, 510 ships totaling 77,250 tons. The term *ton* was used to indicate the size of ships. For cargo vessels a ton meant about 100 cubic feet of interior space. Warships were measured in terms of how many tons of water their hulls would displace when fully loaded. In other words, if the interior space below the waterline of a warship was large enough for 500 tons of water, the ship was called a 500-tonner.

Included in this immense fleet would be all the available galleons, plus forty galleys—warships powered by oars—and six galleasses—a new kind of warship combining oars and sails. Some thirty thousand sailors would be required to sail to England and put an army of fifty thousand soldiers ashore. Once the army was ashore, the fleet would defend it from attack by sea. When the army began to march toward London, galleys and other small ships would support the troops by moving inland using rivers.

The Spanish galleon was a mainstay of the powerful Spanish Armada.

An Expensive Proposition

Santa Cruz planned every last detail of the invasion, from the size of the ships' guns to the number of shoes and dinner plates needed by the soldiers. It could all be done, he wrote, for about four million ducats. Philip did not make notes in the margin of Santa Cruz's plan, but he must have been stunned. Such an amount was equal to all his revenue from the Americas for three years.

Parma's plan was equally simple but not nearly as expensive. His Army of Flanders, sixty thousand strong, was in the Netherlands, just a short distance from England across the English Channel. Parma proposed that a fleet of flat-bottomed barges be assembled in secrecy at one of the coastal cities and used to ferry an army of thirty thousand foot soldiers and five hundred cavalry troops across the channel in a single night. Once ashore, the army would march quickly on London and take it by surprise.

Parma proposed that a screen of only twenty-five warships be used to escort the barges. As for the rest of the Spanish navy, the duke said that only if details of the invasion leaked out should the navy play a role. Perhaps, he wrote, it could

> sail suddenly up here in order to assist and reinforce the troops who have already landed [in Kent in southeastern England] and keep open the seaway between the coasts of Flanders and England; or else—if your fleet is large, well-provided, well-armed and well-manned—it could create a diversion which will draw the English fleet away [from the Channel].

The chief element of Parma's plan was surprise, whereas Santa Cruz would depend on overwhelming force. What Parma did not say in his letter to Philip, however, was how he proposed to keep such a huge undertaking secret from the Dutch and from the English, who had a network of spies on the European mainland. Philip saw the difficulty at once. In the margin of the portion of Parma's plan calling for secrecy, the king made the notation "hardly possible."

The Plans Are Combined

Philip now had two plans for the invasion. One was feasible but too expensive; the other was affordable but impractical. Both, however, contained some good features, and so Philip turned them over to his senior adviser, Don Juan de Zúñiga, for his evaluation. Zúñiga suggested taking the best parts of both plans and combining them.

Under Zúñiga's proposal, a large Spanish fleet—but nowhere near as large as Santa Cruz suggested—would land an army in

Ireland. England's forces, both land and naval, would be drawn westward to meet this threat. Then, while the Spanish fleet battled the English navy near Ireland, Parma would make a dash across the Channel with the main invasion force.

It was already June by the time Zúñiga presented his plan to Philip. Zúñiga argued that the plan required so much preparation that it should not be attempted before autumn weather made sailing conditions in the Atlantic and in the English Channel uncertain. He suggested the invasion be set for August or September 1587. Philip agreed and on July 26 sent full details of the plan to Parma in the Netherlands and Santa Cruz in Lisbon. Neither was invited to make suggestions, only preparations.

Letters soon began to pour from El Escorial to all parts of Spain and to Portugal, Naples, and Sicily, ordering that ships, troops, arms, and supplies be prepared for shipment to Spanish ports where the *Felissima* [most fortunate] *Armada Invencible* was to be assembled. Philip demanded that the pope, Sixtus V, make good on his promise of financial support, and a figure of one million ducats was agreed on. Sixtus, however, had doubts as to whether the invasion was possible. He would make no payment until Spanish soldiers actually set foot on English soil.

The so-called Grand Design for the Enterprise of England had two flaws that were to prove fatal. First, neither Zúñiga nor Philip said how Santa Cruz and Parma, separated by a thousand miles of ocean, were to keep in contact so that the proper timing could take place. Second, and more important, nowhere was it explained how Parma's barges were to evade Dutch or English ships small enough to patrol the waters off the Netherlands coast, waters too shallow for the heavy Spanish warships. Perhaps Philip and Zúñiga did not realize how serious these questions were. On the other hand, perhaps they simply left it to the commanders to find answers.

Philip II made plans to invade England using his newly organized Spanish Armada.

Philip's Demands

Philip had no intention of trying to add England to his empire. Parma was having enough difficulty conquering the Netherlands with sixty thousand troops. Far more would be required to maintain Spanish rule in England. Instead, Philip was prepared to demand three concessions from Elizabeth. First, Catholics would be free to worship openly rather than in secret. Second, all English troops would be withdrawn from the Netherlands. Third, England would be made to pay the expenses of the invasion, and a Spanish army would remain in England until full payment was received.

Philip probably had no wish to remove Elizabeth altogether. He still feared that Mary, Queen of Scots, Elizabeth's lawful heir, would become an ally of France.

Elizabeth herself removed this possibility. In the summer of 1586, a plot against Elizabeth's life by a young Catholic named Anthony Babington was discovered. Mary, Queen of Scots, had been foolhardy enough to write letters of support to Babington. The letters were intercepted, and Mary was tried and convicted. Elizabeth's councillors and most of her subjects demanded that Mary be executed.

Elizabeth delayed and tried to avoid a decision, even suggesting that she would not be too disappointed if Mary were quietly assassinated. At last, however, she gave in, and Mary was beheaded at Fotheringhay Castle on February 12, 1587. In Mary's will, she named Philip as heir to her title to the throne of England.

Mary, Queen of Scots, is beheaded for treason.

Her death, therefore, gave Philip a legitimate—at least in the eyes of all Catholics—excuse to invade England and also removed the threat of an English alliance with France.

England was fully aware of Spain's plans. In the spring of 1587, Sir Francis Drake, whom the Spaniards feared more than any other English sailor and whom they called El Draque (the Dragon) convinced Sir Francis Walsingham, Elizabeth's secretary, that instead of waiting for the Armada to attack, the English should do everything possible to disrupt its formation. Walsingham, in turn, managed to convince a very reluctant Elizabeth to allow Drake to "singe the king of Spain's beard" in a raid.

Just in Time

Drake knew his queen well, especially her tendency to change her mind. On April 11, only two weeks after receiving his orders, he sailed from Plymouth with a north, or "Protestant," wind at his back. "The wind commands me away," he wrote. "Our ship is under sail. God grant we may so live in His fear as the enemy may have cause to say that God doth fight for her Majesty as well abroad as at home."

Drake was right to sail as soon as he did. On April 19, Elizabeth announced she was revoking Drake's orders. A pinnace, or small messenger ship, was sent after him but did not find the English squadron. It may be that Elizabeth never intended to stop Drake at all, but only wished to be able to tell Philip that she had tried to prevent the raid.

From the captain of a captured Portuguese ship, Drake knew that while Santa Cruz and the bulk of the Spanish fighting fleet was in Lisbon, the southern harbor of Cádiz was full of merchant shipping protected only by galleys. On the afternoon of April 29, his squadron reached the entrance to the bay. Without even waiting for the hindmost of his twenty-five ships to catch up, he summoned what captains were on hand to a council aboard his flagship, the *Elizabeth Bonaventure*.

Drake's second-in-command, William Borough, urged his admiral to wait for the other captains and then draw up a plan, possibly waiting until morning to attack. Drake, however, was a man of action. "The advantage of time and place in martial actions is half a victory," he once wrote. He told Borough the attack would begin at once. Before Borough had even reached his own ship, the *Golden Lion*, Drake was headed into Cádiz harbor under full sail. The rest of his fleet followed as quickly as it could.

Don Pedro de Acuña, commander of the galleys defending the harbor, tried to fight, but it was an unequal contest. Galleys were built only to fight other galleys, either by ramming or by grappling and boarding. Their guns were mounted only on the bow (front) and stern (rear), the sides being taken up with oars.

Seizing the moment, Francis Drake attacks the Spanish in Cádiz harbor.

The much heavier English galleons swept past them, delivering broadsides from the guns that lined their sides. Finally, the galleys, their decks filled with the dead or dying, limped into a shallow area of the harbor where the galleons could not follow.

A Harbor Ablaze

The English next turned to the merchantmen, or cargo ships, in the harbor. Some of the smaller ships had run for shallow water, but the larger ones were helpless. Many did not even have their crews aboard. Drake selected the ships he wanted to take as prizes. The rest were unloaded of any useful cargo and then burned. Night had fallen, but the glow of the burning vessels cast a glow over the city.

The English might have captured the city itself, but the duke of Medina Sidonia rode in the next day with a force of about six thousand men. Medina Sidonia managed to reorganize the defenses of Cádiz, positioning guns onshore so that they could do some damage to the English, who at last sailed away on May 1. Later, a confidential list of the damage made for King Philip showed that twenty-four ships had been captured or burned. "The loss was not very great," Philip said, "but the daring of the attempt was very great indeed."

Drake's daring, however, had just begun. After capturing the town of Sagres on Cape Saint Vincent at the southwestern tip of Spain, Drake made it a base from which he preyed on ships from the Mediterranean that were attempting to join Santa Cruz.

Drake's work over these weeks was unexciting but very important. He destroyed fishing villages up and down the coast, even burning boats and nets to deny the Armada a source of food supplies. He captured a series of small boats loaded with "hoops and pipe staves [small wooden planks] and such like . . . above 16 or 17 hundred tons in weight" that he piled onshore and burned. These were materials for making barrels in which the food and water for the Armada would be stored. Thanks to Drake, the Spanish were eventually forced to use green, unseasoned wood for their barrels, which caused the food to spoil and the water to grow foul.

On May 31, the English fleet sailed from Cape Saint Vincent bound, Drake said, for the Azores. Instead, he intercepted a Portuguese merchantman, the *San Felipe*, heading toward Lisbon from India with a cargo of spices, silk cloth, ivory, gold, and silver. Drake captured the *San Felipe* after a brief fight and carried

The Reluctant Commander

When the duke of Medina Sidonia received a letter from King Philip appointing him Captain General of the Ocean Sea and supreme commander of the Spanish Armada, the duke was stunned and dismayed. He had no wish for such an appointment and told his king so, as these excerpts from his famous letter show:

> I first humbly thank His Majesty for having thought of me for so great a task, and I wish I possessed the talents and strength necessary for it. But, sir, I have not health for the sea, for I know by the small experience I have had afloat that I soon become sea-sick and have many humours [unpleasant feelings]. Besides this . . . I am in great need, so much so that when I have had to go to Madrid I have been obliged to borrow money for the journey. . . . Apart from this, neither my conscience nor my duty will allow me to take this service upon me. The force [the Armada] is so great, and the undertaking so important that it would not be right for a person like myself, possessing no experience of seafaring or war, to take charge of it. So, sir, in the interest of His Majesty's service, and for the love I bear him, I submit to you . . . that I possess neither aptitude, ability, health, nor fortune for the expedition. . . . But besides all this, for me to take charge of the Armada afresh, without the slightest knowledge of it, of the persons who are to take part in it, of the objects in view, of the intelligence from England, without any acquaintance with the ports there, or of the arrangements which the Marquis [the late admiral Santa Cruz] has been making for years past, would be simply groping in the dark. . . . So, sir, you will see that my reasons for declining are so strong and convincing in His Majesty's own interests, that I cannot attempt a task of which I have no doubt I should give a bad account.

For centuries, mostly because of this letter, historians blamed Medina Sidonia for the defeat of the Armada. Later historians, however, have argued that the duke did as good a job or better than anyone else could have done, and that the real blame should go to King Philip for proceeding with an invasion plan that was seriously flawed to begin with.

the riches back to England. Her cargo was worth £114,000, three times the combined value of the ships Drake had taken at Cádiz.

An Extra Year for England

Despite the destruction he had wrought, the greatest harm done by Drake was yet to come. King Philip, thinking Drake was bound for the Azores to intercept the Spanish treasure fleet, ordered Santa Cruz to take whatever warships were ready and sail to the Azores to protect the fleet. Santa Cruz saw the treasure safely back to Spain, but it was September 25 when he returned. His voyage had consumed not only time, but also supplies.

Francis Drake's tricky maneuvering against the Spanish allowed him both to seize treasure for Elizabeth and to send the Spanish Armada on a fool's errand to the Azores.

Philip wanted the Armada to sail immediately despite the shortages and the approach of fierce autumn weather. To speed things up, he even changed the entire plan for the invasion. For more than a year, Parma had been writing to the king, expressing doubt about Zúñiga's plan for a two-stage invasion. He urged instead that the Armada sail directly for the Dutch coast to ensure that Parma's army could cross the English Channel in safety.

Philip finally agreed, and on September 14, 1587, issued his new plan to Parma, writing:

> I have decided that as soon as the marquis of Santa Cruz [returns] he will pick up the rest of the fleet that awaits him and they will all sail directly, in the name of God, to the English Channel . . . until they drop anchor off Margate Head [the southeastern tip of England]. . . . You will be so prepared that when you see the narrow seas thus secured . . . you will immediately send the whole army over in the boats you have prepared.

The key questions remained unanswered. Were Parma's barges supposed to meet the Armada on the open sea? If so, how were they to get past the sea beggars' cromsters, commanded by Justin of Nassau, son of William of Orange? If the Armada was to escort Parma's barges past the blockade, how would it navigate the shallow water and sandbars?

From the moment he landed in Lisbon, Santa Cruz was bombarded with letters from Philip urging him to hurry. The admiral replied in vain that the danger of bad weather was too great. "We are quite aware of the risk . . . ," the king replied, "but since it all is for His cause, God will send good weather." Philip demanded the Armada sail no later than October 25. Santa Cruz did the best he could, but at age sixty-two was not physically up to the task. Besides, he was a fighter, not an organizer. October turned to November and then to December. Finally in January, even though Santa Cruz assured him the Armada would be fit to sail by the end of the month, Philip decided to find out for himself. He sent the count of Fuentes to Lisbon to examine the situation and, if need be, to remove Santa Cruz from office.

Fuentes found a disorderly muddle. Food supplies were rotting on piers. Ships had been equipped with guns but not with the proper size shot. Guns were on hand for which there were no carriages. Men were deserting by the hundreds. Clearly, Santa Cruz had made a mess of things, but it was unnecessary for Fuentes to remove him. Spain's most famous admiral died, worn out by his efforts, on February 9.

A New Commander

Santa Cruz's death posed a problem to Philip. Spain had several seasoned seamen—Juan Martínez de Recalde, Don Miguel de Oquendo, Don Pedro de Valdés, Don Diego Flores de Valdés, Don Hugo de Moncada—but there was no obvious choice to succeed Santa Cruz. For one thing, to elevate any one of them to supreme command would make the others jealous. For another, Spain was extremely class-conscious. The commander of so great an undertaking as the Armada must be of such noble birth that members of the best families would not refuse to serve under him.

Philip's choice was Don Alonso Pérez de Guzmán el Bueno, duke of Medina Sidonia—the same man who had ridden to rescue Cádiz from Drake the previous year. In some ways, it was a logical appointment. Medina Sidonia (a duke was customarily known by the name of his duchy rather than by his own name) was thirty-eight years old and head of one of Spain's most ancient families. He was a talented administrator and had been heavily involved in the planning of the Armada. But, although he was an experienced soldier, he had no knowledge of sea warfare. His only experience had been outfitting for expeditions to the Americas.

When he received Philip's letter naming him Captain General of the Ocean Sea, Medina Sidonia was horrified. He immediately wrote to the king seeking to escape the appointment. He was in debt, he said, and could not afford to leave his estates. He had "no experience of seafaring or war." He had no knowledge of English seaports and would be "groping in the dark." Besides, he wrote, he tended to get seasick.

The king would have none of it. "It is I who must judge your capabilities," he wrote, "and I am fully satisfied with these." Medina Sidonia had no choice. Sorrowfully, he left his estate at San Lúcar with its cherished orange groves and headed for Lisbon.

Bringing Order from Chaos

When he arrived, he found a situation even worse than Fuentes had discovered in January. Nothing had been done since Santa Cruz's death. Many of the 108 ships in the harbor were in various states of disrepair. Within a few months, Medina Sidonia had proved the wisdom of Philip's choice. The number of ships grew to 130, all of them seaworthy. Troop strength went from twelve thousand to nineteen thousand. Ships' guns of varying sizes, which had been gathered from all over Europe, were matched with the proper shot. The Armada was almost ready to sail.

The Armada might never have sailed at all if Drake had had his way. Ever since November 1587 he had been pleading with Queen Elizabeth to allow him to launch a raid on Lisbon. "Wherefore, if your Majesty would command me away with these ships which are here [at Plymouth] already, and the rest to follow with all possible expedition, I hold it in my opinion the surest and best course."

Elizabeth, however, still hoped to avoid a war altogether. She kept the fleet in port and even ordered the crews disbanded so that she would not have to pay them. She entered into negotiations with Parma in Flanders, hoping to win a compromise with Philip. While the Armada sat helpless in Lisbon, Drake sat frustrated in Plymouth.

It was far too late for King Philip to compromise. He had spent a fortune readying the Armada for sea. He had proclaimed the Enterprise of England before the world as his holy cause. If he backed down now, he would look foolish. The Armada must sail.

On April 25, the fleet was dedicated at a great service in Lisbon cathedral. As Medina Sidonia knelt at the altar and guns fired a salute, the archbishop placed in his hands one corner of a huge banner that had been blessed by the pope. It showed the symbol of the royal house of Spain flanked by a crucified Christ and the Virgin Mary. Beneath were the words "Arise, O Lord, and vindicate thy cause."

Drake's Impatience

Sir Francis Drake was a man of action. When he saw an opportunity, as he did during his raid on Cádiz in 1587, he seldom waited for anyone to agree with him before plunging ahead.

In the spring of 1588, however, he was forced to stay put when he was convinced that by striking quickly at the Armada while it was in port at Lisbon, he could prevent it from ever sailing against England. To sail against Spain, he needed permission from Queen Elizabeth, who—as usual—was unwilling to make a decision.

Frustrated, Drake bombarded Elizabeth's council with letters, all of them urging immediate action. One read:

> If there may be such a stay or stop made by any means of this fleet in Spain so that they may not come through the seas as conquerors—which I assure myself they think to do—then shall the Prince of Parma have such a check thereby as were meet. . . . My very good lords, next under God's mighty protection, the advantage again of time and place will be the only and chief means for our good; wherein I most humbly beseech your good Lordships to persevere as you have begun; for that with fifty sails of shipping we shall do more good upon their own coasts than a great deal more will do here at home.

When his letters to her council brought no results, Drake wrote directly to the queen, "The advantage of time and place in all martial [military] actions is half the victory, which being lost is irrecoverable. Wherefore, if your Majesty will command me away. . . ." In another letter, he implored Elizabeth:

> I beseech you to pardon my boldness in the discharge of my conscience, being burdened to signify unto your Highness the imminent dangers that in my simple opinion do hang over us. . . . The promise of peace from the Prince of Parma [with whom Elizabeth was negotiating at the time] and these mighty preparations in Spain agree not well together.

Finally, Drake visited Elizabeth in person and convinced her to move the main part of the Royal Navy to Plymouth. By the time the fleet under Lord Howard arrived, however, the Armada had already sailed from Lisbon. Drake and Howard did set forth on a raid against the Armada when it was in the port of Corunna but were blown back by contrary winds.

Sir Francis Drake's philosophy of seizing the moment conflicted with Elizabeth I's caution.

FRANCISCVS DRAECK · NOBILISSIMVS EQVES ANGLIAE · IS EST QVI TOTO T TERRARVM ORBE CRCMDVGO

jd circůmdůcto pernosco in fonqiúdine, in latitudine est impossibile, etc:

A Catholic priest blesses the Armada before it sails for England. Philip believed that God would be on his side and grant him a victory.

Philip was confident God would provide a victory. Others were not so sure. The pope received a report from an agent who had talked with an anonymous Spanish officer, who said sarcastically,

> Unless God helps us by a miracle, the English, who have faster and handier ships than ours, and many more long-range guns, and who know their advantage just as well as we do, will never close [draw near] with us at all, but will stand aloof and knock us to pieces with their culverins [large guns], without our being able to do them any serious hurt. So, we are sailing against England in the confident hope of a miracle.

On May 28, the mighty Armada weighed anchor at Lisbon and sailed down the Tagus River toward the open sea. The night before, a Spanish observer had written, "All wars and affairs are reduced to this one enterprise."

CHAPTER THREE

Through the Channel

The goal of the Spanish Armada was simple—to sail through the English Channel to Flanders and link up with Parma's army. The goal of the English fleet also was simple—to prevent the Spaniards from doing so. But although the English were to hold their own in a week-long series of battles, they failed to inflict any serious damage on the Armada, which drew ever nearer to its objective.

When it had become evident in April 1588 that the Armada would sail, Queen Elizabeth finally agreed to allow her fleet to prepare for the invasion. Drake had won at least one concession. Instead of concentrating on the narrow seas between Flanders and England, the fleet was to form at Plymouth on the south-western coast. Drake had argued that since the Armada had to come through the Channel, the English should meet it as far west as possible and do everything they could to stop it.

The supreme commander of Elizabeth's fleet, however, was not Drake. Although England was not as class-conscious as Spain, a highborn commander still was necessary, and Elizabeth would have stirred jealousy among other captains by putting Drake in charge. Fortunately for the queen, she had an obvious choice—Lord Howard of Effingham, who had been named Lord Admiral of the Royal Navy in 1585. Although his experience in sea warfare was nothing like Drake's, he came from a family of sailors and was the fourth member of his family to hold the title of Lord Admiral. Furthermore, he was a cousin of the queen.

Drake had been at Plymouth with his squadron since February. On June 3 he was joined by Howard along with most of the

Lord Howard of Effingham, Lord Admiral of the Royal Navy.

English fleet. Only a squadron commanded by Lord Henry Seymour was left guarding the passage between Flanders and England. On reaching Plymouth, Howard made Drake his vice admiral. It does not appear that Drake resented not being in full command or that Howard resented Drake's greater fame.

Drake was not Howard's only talented captain. John Hawkins, England's first great sailor and Drake's former superior, commanded part of the fleet. Also serving under Howard was Martin Frobisher, a tough Yorkshire man and a bitter rival of Drake. Frobisher had made three voyages to what is now Canada, seeking the Northwest Passage to Asia. He explored much of northeastern Canada, and a bay in Baffin Island bears his name.

In Port Once More

Meanwhile, the Armada was slowly making its way north. On June 19, after two weeks of battling northerly winds, Medina Sidonia had only come as far as Cape Finisterre, the northwestern corner of Spain. So many of his supplies had been consumed that he was forced to head for the Spanish port of Corunna to obtain more. Furthermore, a sudden storm had scattered the fleet, and some ships took as long as two weeks to reach Corunna.

Explorer Martin Frobisher (above) was Drake's bitter rival. (Below) The Spanish Armada enters the English Channel to battle the English navy.

Drake had finally convinced both Howard and Queen Elizabeth that England's best chance for victory was to surprise the Armada while in port. The English fleet sailed for Corunna on July 17, but two days later the wind changed and blew from the south. The English were forced back to Plymouth, reaching port on July 22. The day before, the Armada used the same wind to leave Corunna and head for the Channel.

On Friday, July 29, the Armada sighted the Lizard, as the point at the southwestern tip of England is called. Medina Sidonia ordered the fleet to anchor and called a war council aboard his flagship, the *San Martín*. The Spaniards knew that Drake and at least some of the English fleet were at Plymouth, about forty-five miles northeast, and some officers, particularly the headstrong, young Don Alonso Martínez de Leiva, one of King Philip's personal favorites, wanted to attack immediately. No, Medina Sidonia told them, his orders from King Philip were to sail directly to the Netherlands. Reluctantly, the others agreed, and the Armada headed slowly east, passing up what would have been its best chance to destroy the English fleet.

Drake and Howard, however, were alert to the danger. Thomas Fleming in one of the small English ships patrolling the Channel had spotted the Armada and sailed to Plymouth, arriving there late on the afternoon of the twenty-ninth. The story goes that he found Drake bowling on a lawn and rushed up to deliver his message. "There is plenty of time to finish the game and beat the Spaniards, too," the English admiral is supposed to have said.

The English Sail

Whether Drake finished his game or not, he or Howard most certainly ordered the fleet to make immediate preparations to sail. They knew everything might be lost if the Armada trapped them inside Plymouth harbor. At 10 P.M., the English ships began leaving Plymouth on an outgoing tide, battling a southwesterly wind. By the morning of the thirtieth, the entire fleet was in the Channel heading west. Even though the English had escaped the harbor, the Spaniards had the advantage of holding the "weather gauge." That is, when the fleets met, the wind would be at the Armada's back, making it far easier for the Spanish ships to maneuver.

Late in the day, the Spaniards were able to see the English fleet on the eastern horizon. Medina Sidonia was afraid to continue eastward. He did not want to pass the English during the night and let his opponents gain the weather gauge. The Armada dropped anchor and waited to attack when dawn came.

The next morning, the duke received a shock. During the night, most of the English fleet had sailed across the front of the Armada to the south and then swung back around to the northwest. One squadron had tacked—taken a zigzag course—around

Sir John Hawkins

If Sir Francis Drake was the Englishman most feared by Spaniards, John Hawkins was not far behind. He made a name for himself in the 1560s, buying or stealing slaves from Portuguese Africa and then selling them to Spanish settlers in America, often threatening to burn down their towns if they didn't buy his cargo. He was known in America and throughout the Spanish fleet as Juan Achines.

Hawkins came from a well-to-do ship-owning family in Plymouth. His father had made several nice profits for King Henry VIII, so it was only natural that Henry's daughter, Elizabeth I, should invest when Hawkins decided to test King Philip II of Spain's toleration of English trading in Spanish America.

Hawkins's first three voyages were successful, but the fourth, when he was ambushed by Spanish ships at San Juan de Ulúa in Mexico, almost cost him his life. Despite his actions against Spain, he claimed to be a friend of Philip and even participated in a Spanish plot against Elizabeth in 1571. Actually, however, he was keeping his queen and her council advised of the plotters' actions, and all were eventually arrested. Partially in reward, Elizabeth named him Treasurer of the Navy in 1578.

At the time, the Royal Navy was led by a board made up of four principal officers. Hawkins discovered that not only the members of the board, but also officials at every level, had been pilfering supplies and making claims for false expenses in order to line their own pockets. He reformed the way the navy was financed, promising to do everything for a fixed yearly sum.

His greatest contribution was in his design for the new ships of the Royal Navy built during his administration. His sleek, fast, "race-built" ships were by far the finest in either fleet when the English battled the Armada.

Hawkins continued to play a leading role in the Royal Navy. His last voyage was once more to the Americas with Drake. By this time, however, he was sixty-three years old and in poor health. The expedition had barely reached the Caribbean when Hawkins became ill. He died on November 12, 1595, and was buried at sea.

Originally making his name as a smuggler of slaves, Sir John Hawkins would later greatly improve the design of the Royal Navy's ships.

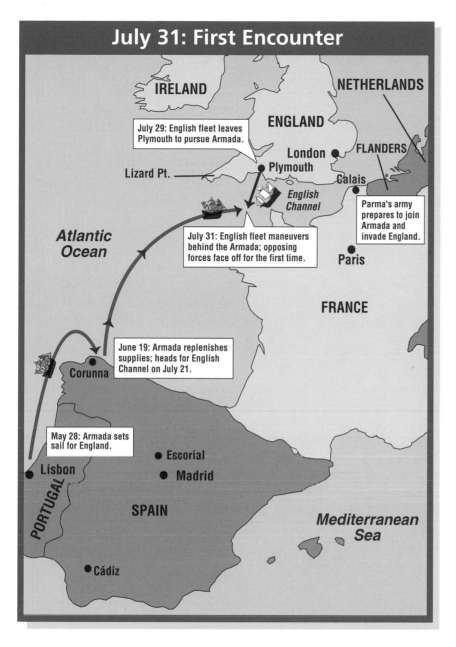

July 31: First Encounter

July 29: English fleet leaves Plymouth to pursue Armada.

IRELAND

NETHERLANDS

ENGLAND

London

Plymouth

FLANDERS

Lizard Pt.

Calais

English Channel

Parma's army prepares to join Armada and invade England.

Atlantic Ocean

July 31: English fleet maneuvers behind the Armada; opposing forces face off for the first time.

Paris

FRANCE

June 19: Armada replenishes supplies; heads for English Channel on July 21.

Corunna

May 28: Armada sets sail for England.

Escorial

Lisbon

Madrid

PORTUGAL

SPAIN

Mediterranean Sea

Cádiz

the northern wing of the Armada. As a result, the English held the weather gauge when the sun rose on July 31 and the fleets faced one another for the first time.

Medina Sidonia was not the only one shocked by what he saw that morning. The English could see for the first time the extent of the Spanish fleet. "We never thought," wrote one English observer, "that they could ever have found, gathered and joined so great a force of puissant [strong] ships together and so well appointed them with their cannon, culverin, and other great pieces of brass ordinance [guns]."

Of the 130 ships that had sailed from Lisbon, only 5 had not reached England. The 4 galleys could not stand up to the rough

The Game of Bowls

Perhaps the most famous of all stories connected with the Spanish Armada is that of Thomas Fleming, the sailor who first spotted the Spaniards and rushed to Plymouth with the news and found Sir Francis Drake and Lord Howard bowling on Plymouth Hoe, an open, grassy area overlooking the harbor. Drake is supposed to have replied to Fleming's message that there was "plenty of time to finish the game and beat the Spaniards, too."

Whether Drake actually made such a comment has never been proved. The bowling story first appeared in a pamphlet printed in England in 1624 and was then said to have been told by people "well within living memory of the event." While the 1624 story describes the bowling game, it makes no mention of the famous comment by Drake.

It was not until a century after the pamphlet was printed that the first report of Drake's comment appears. But while it appears that the story may be nothing more than a patriotic legend, it may have gotten its start as being just the kind of thing Drake might have said to prevent a panic throughout the English fleet.

Some historians have argued that Drake's comment does not make sense, because no time was to be wasted getting the English fleet out of Plymouth harbor before it could be trapped by the Armada. All that would have been necessary, however, is for Drake and Howard to give the necessary orders. They knew the tide would not be favorable for a departure until about 10 P.M. and thus did, indeed, have plenty of time to finish the game.

It is also interesting that the name of Fleming's pinnace was the *Golden Hind*, the same name as the ship in which Drake had sailed around the world years earlier.

In a painting titled The Armada in Sight, *Drake bowls at Plymouth harbor while the Armada is spotted on the horizon.*

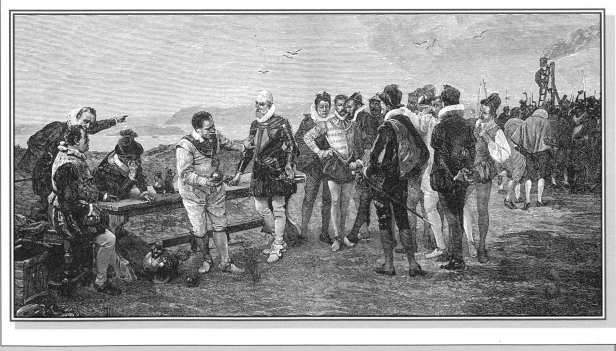

In this depiction of a Spanish galleon, the unwieldy stern castle can clearly be seen.

Atlantic seas, and 1 armed merchant ship had lost a mast and fled for shore. Still, it was the largest fleet the world had ever known. There were 64 prime fighting ships, either galleons or heavily armed merchantmen, 25 *urcas*, or cargo ships, and 32 *pataches* and *zabras*, small, swift vessels used for scouting or communications. Also present were 4 galleasses, the ships combining sails and oars that the Spaniards hoped would be more maneuverable than the English ships.

A total of 197 English ships are listed as having participated in the Armada campaign, but most of these were supply ships that shuttled back and forth between the fleet and the shore. Others were pinnaces, the English version of the *zabras*. The heart of the English fleet consisted of the 21 frontline ships of the Royal Navy and about 40 armed merchant ships. In numbers of fighting ships, therefore, the two sides were about equal.

Types of Ships

More important than the number of ships, however, were their sailing qualities. Because large amounts of supplies were needed for long voyages, Spanish ships were built wider across the beam—the widest part of the ship—to provide cargo space. This width, as the ship plowed through the water, made it clumsy and gave it a tendency to wallow from side to side.

The Spanish ships also featured "castles," large, multistoried structures at the bow and stern. The castles were intended as places from which soldiers could fire arrows or muskets down on their opponents when coming alongside. Since they rose so far up from the deck, however, the castles acted like unwanted sails, catching the wind and making the ship that much harder to maneuver.

The English could trace the superiority of their ships to Queen Elizabeth's father, Henry VIII, who was able to see that the best defense for his country was a fleet of ships that could be mobilized quickly for short voyages and close-to-home fighting. By 1546, he had founded the Royal Navy and began a program of shipbuilding. The castles of English ships were much smaller because Henry, a great student of guns and artillery, foresaw a time when sea battles would be won not by hand-to-hand fighting between soldiers, but by long-range guns. Under Henry's guidance, the English developed the practice of placing along a ship's side rows of guns that, in battle, were extended through gun ports, or windows. Henry saw that the "broadside," the firing of these guns at the same moment, would be a formidable weapon.

Henry's innovations were improved when John Hawkins became Treasurer of the Navy in 1578. Before Henry VIII, the main function of ships had been to carry soldiers. Under Henry, the ship became a weapon to be used in combination with the soldiers aboard. Under Hawkins, the ship itself was the primary weapon. Sails were improved, and most of the guns were designed to damage other ships at long distances, not to kill the men on board them. From Hawkins's time on, English ships were "race-built," much longer in relation to their width than before

An English ship shows the features that made her clearly superior to the Spanish galleon. The ship is narrower, with gun ports along her sides.

The English Advantage

Lord Howard's flagship, the Ark Royal, *displays the advantages over the Spanish ships.*

The advantages of the English ships and guns over those of the Armada were enumerated shortly after the battle by Sir Arthur Gorgas. Gorgas admitted that the Spaniards held the edge in "hugeness and numbers of their vessels as for multitude of soldiers and mariners," but went on to say that the English nevertheless held an overall advantage

as namely for our swiftness in outsailing them, our nimbleness in getting into the weather [windward] of them, our little draught [depth of the hull below the waterline] of them, our stout bearing up of our sides in all huge winds when theirs must stoop to their great disadvantage many ways, our yawness [maneuverability] in staying well and casting about twice for their once and so discharging our broadsides or ordnance [gunnery] twice for their single, we carrying as good and great artillery as they do and to better proof and having far better gunners, our knowledge and pilotage of our own coasts, channels, sands and harbours, and soundings [water depth] being far above theirs. . . . I say, setting the one against the other for a seafight [we] are more powerful to annoy them and guard our coasts than they of force to offend and invade us if we use the benefit of our shipping right, and God give us grace to employ these gifts to the best purpose. . . . For without his grace, his gifts do little avail in any human course whatsoever.

since not as much space was needed for cargo or men. They were far more maneuverable than any sailing ship the world had known. Early in 1588, Howard reported to Lord Burghley, Elizabeth's principal minister:

> I protest it before God, if it were not for her Majesty's presence I had rather live in the company of these noble ships than in any place. . . . I have been aboard of every ship that goeth out with me, and in every place where any may creep . . . and there is never a one of them that knows what a leak means. . . . There is none that goeth out now but I durst [would dare] go to the Rio de la Plata [a river in Argentina] in her.

Guns and Carriages

The ships of the Spanish Armada carried 2,431 guns among them, but more than half were smaller than four-pounders (so called because of the weight of the cannonballs they fired) and would be useless except at very short range. Since the Spaniards' basic strategy was the ancient Mediterranean style of naval warfare—grappling and boarding—a large percentage of their guns were short-range cannons designed to kill the men on board enemy ships or to damage sails and rigging. The Spaniards had some large-caliber guns, but many were intended for use on land against city walls and were too large and unwieldy for shipboard use.

Sailors rally aboard a Spanish galleon as an English ship approaches. Because the Armada's guns were inferior to those of the English fleet, Spanish sailors were prepared to board enemy ships and fight the English hand-to-hand.

The English guns, on the other hand, were heavier and designed to damage opponents' ships at long range. The total number of guns in the English fleet is unknown, but one expert estimated that it had 1,972 guns heavier than four-pounders. Of these, 1,874 or 95 percent were long-range pieces. Howard and Drake were determined to avoid a battle at close quarters, where their ships' decks would be swept by Spanish guns. Their strategy was to stand off from the Armada and try to pound it to pieces with their longer range artillery.

Just as important to the English as the types of guns used were the carriages, or platforms, on which they were mounted. Spanish gun carriages were designed for use on land, with two large wheels and a long "trail" behind that could be hitched to horses for overland transportation. The length of the trails made it difficult for the guns to be handled in such a confined space as a ship's deck. The English gun carriages were especially designed for warships. The guns were set on box-shaped carriages with four small wheels, or "trucks." These compact carriages were far easier to bring in after each shot, reload, and run out again through the gun ports.

There also were important differences between the Englishmen and Spaniards who sailed the ships and manned the guns. The Spaniards far outnumbered the English—30,656 to 15,925—but almost 19,000 of the men of the Armada were soldiers whose numbers would matter in a sea battle only if it were fought hand-to-hand. Since there were only about 8,000 trained sailors in the Armada, soldiers had to be used in working the ship and guns, tasks they were unused to.

An International Fleet

Another problem for the Armada was that it was "Spanish" in name only. The ships and their crews came from Spain, Portugal, Naples, and Sicily. Only about eight thousand men were actually Spaniards, the others being Italians, Portuguese, Burgundians, Irish, Scottish, Belgians, and Germans. This led to confusion in everything from communication to different measurements for guns and shot.

In comparison, the English were all countrymen and almost all were experienced sailors. There was little class distinction on board the English ships, and Drake made it a rule that gentlemen should "haul and draw"—the manual labor of sailing—along with the common seamen. As a result, ships' companies worked much more as a unit than their Spanish counterparts and were much more efficient in sailing and gunnery.

These, then, were the fleets facing one another on July 31. The English were in a line about nine miles long stretching north and south. The Spaniards adopted a formation the English had

A typical sailor under Drake's command. English sailors felt more loyalty to their captain and country than did their Spanish counterparts. (Below) The English fire the first shot against the Spanish.

never seen. Their ships formed a huge crescent six miles long, the points extending toward the English fleet. The hulks, or cargo ships, were in the center, protected by a strong squadron under Medina Sidonia. The northern wing, closest to land, was commanded by Recalde and the seaward wing by Leiva. Since the points of the crescent were the most vulnerable to attack, some of the strongest ships were stationed there.

The battle started with a gesture right out of the Middle Ages—the formal challenge. Howard sent his own pinnace—appropriately named the *Disdain*—sailing into the middle of the crescent. Firing a single shot from its tiny gun at Medina Sidonia's flagship, it wheeled about and scuttled back to safety.

Almost immediately, the English attacked—Howard against Leiva and Drake against Recalde. Their tactics were new to the Spaniards and, indeed, new to naval warfare. The classic attack formation was "in-line abreast" with ships moving side by side toward the enemy. Instead, the English sailed "in-line astern." The lead ship, usually that of the commander, swept across an enemy's front, the remainder of his ships trailing behind in single file, firing broadsides as they passed.

The Spaniards Fight Back

At the southern end of the crescent, Leiva and his squadron turned to meet the attack. Howard, leading in the *Ark Royal*, kept his ships well away from the Spaniards, and although both sides fired round after round, the range was too long for much damage to be done.

At the opposite end, Recalde in the *San Juan de Portugal* likewise turned to meet Drake. Only one ship in his squadron, however, *El Gran Grin*, followed him. The rest continued to sail east, leaving the two galleons isolated. Quickly, the English, including Drake and Frobisher, surrounded Recalde. Some historians have

A painting depicts the action on board Lord Howard's Ark Royal *as it fights Don Alonso de Leiva's ship.*

charged that the veteran Recalde did this on purpose, hoping to lure the English into a general battle at close quarters. If this is so, he failed. Drake maintained a range of about three hundred yards and pounded the Spaniards with his longer range guns.

Finally Medina Sidonia, seeing Recalde in trouble, sped to the rescue in the *San Martín*, the rest of his squadron following. He was able to reach Recalde and force the English to withdraw to a safer range. The battle went on for about two more hours—always at a distance—until Howard, whose fleet still had not reached full strength, ordered a withdrawal.

Only after the shooting stopped was any real damage done. As the Spaniards attempted to re-form, Pedro de Valdés in the *Rosario* collided with another ship and lost his bowsprit, the wooden spar extending forward from the bow to which the stays of the foremast were fastened. At about the same time, a huge explosion rocked the *San Salvador*. The entire stern castle was torn out, the masts were broken, and two hundred crewmen were killed.

Medina Sidonia sailed back to try to save both ships. He was able to take some of the wounded off the *San Salvador* and managed to get a line attached to the *Rosario* to tow her back to the fleet. The line snapped, however, and Medina Sidonia was convinced by Diego Flores de Valdés, his second-in-command and Pedro's cousin, to abandon both crippled ships.

Standoff at Sea

The first battle was over, and neither side had any right to be joyful. The Spaniards were amazed by the sailing ability of the English ships and knew that as long as the English held the weather gauge, the battle would be fought on Howard's terms. The English, though, had not managed to inflict any damage on the Armada with their long-range guns, and the Spaniards, as night fell, resumed their formation and continued up the Channel.

Howard wanted to maintain contact with the Armada. He assigned Drake to lead the English fleet in pursuit of the enemy and to hang a lantern at his stern as a guide. During the night, however, Drake extinguished the light and turned aside to investigate, he said later, "strange sails." Actually, he had gone back in his *Revenge*, along with the *Bear* and the *Mary Rose*, to capture the stricken *Rosario*, which surrendered without a fight.

In later times, to ignore orders and set off after a prize would be an offense for which Drake could have been court-martialed. Now, however, no one seemed too upset by it, except for Frobisher, who later said that unless Drake shared his prize, including fifty-five thousand gold ducats, he would make Drake "spend [lose] the best blood in his belly."

With no light to guide them, most of the English ships "hove to," or stopped. Howard continued eastward with a few ships. Toward

After the shooting ceased, the Armada encountered further hardship. The Rosario, *commanded by Pedro de Valdés (pictured), was damaged during a collision, and an explosion devastated the* San Salvador, *killing two hundred crewmen.*

dawn he saw a light ahead and hurried to catch up, thinking it was Drake. As the sun began to rise, however, he saw that he had sailed almost into the middle of the Spanish fleet. He hurriedly came about (turned around) and sped to rejoin his fleet.

There was no fighting on August 1. The wind was light and variable, and the English were content to shadow the Armada up-channel. Early on the next morning, however, the wind changed and began to blow steadily from the east. For the first time, the Armada had the weather gauge.

The English were the first to realize what had happened. Howard took a northeasterly course, trying to "weather," or sail around, the landward side of the Armada. Medina Sidonia was too quick for him. His squadron cut the English off before they could dart between the Spaniards and the small point of land known as Portland Bill. Seeing he could not get around the Armada to the north, Howard swung around and sailed south-southwest, hoping to weather the southern flank. Once again, he was too late. Spanish squadrons under Leiva and Martín de Bertendona intercepted him, and Howard had no choice but to stand and fight. The Spaniards tried to use their wind advantage to get in close range, intending to grapple and board, but the more maneuverable English ships skipped nimbly out of range.

The English fleet attacks the Armada off Portland Bill.

Frobisher in Trouble

Meanwhile, at the northern end of the battle, Frobisher in the *Triumph*, the largest ship in either fleet at twelve hundred tons, had not followed Howard but had tried to squeeze between Portland Bill and the Armada. He, along with five armed merchantmen, were cut off and had to drop anchor to avoid running aground. Medina Sidonia, seeing Frobisher in trouble, sent the four galleasses commanded by Hugo de Moncada after him.

Now, the wind began to shift to the south. Howard headed north, intending to come to Frobisher's aid, but Frobisher needed no help. Turning his guns on the galleasses' banks of rowers, he killed so many of them that Moncada broke off the fight before Howard could arrive. The galleasses, from which the Spaniards had expected great things, had proved unable to deal with a handful of English ships at anchor.

Drake, meanwhile, had been biding his time. He knew from long experience that east winds in early August mornings tended to shift before too long. When the wind veered to the south, he was ready with his squadron and sailed in to attack Recalde, who soon found himself isolated once again. Medina Sidonia had been leading his squadron to intercept Howard, but when he saw Recalde in trouble, he signaled his ships to go to Recalde's aid and stayed alone to fight Howard. He "struck," or hauled down, the topsails of the *San Martín*, an invitation for Howard to grapple and board. Howard would have none of it. His ships slid by the *San Martín* one at a time, firing broadsides as they passed. For more than an hour, Medina Sidonia fought alone until he was finally rescued by Oquendo's galleons.

At this point, the Spaniards were able to re-form their crescent, and the English withdrew. Again, the battle had been inconclusive. The English had not yet been able to sink a single Spanish ship. The Spaniards had learned that even with the weather gauge, they could not grapple and board the English ships.

There was very little action on Wednesday, August 3. At dawn the English attacked *El Gran Grifón*, a Spanish hulk that had drifted out of position. Recalde, Oquendo, and Bertendona sailed to her rescue, and the English withdrew after a short, sharp gunfight in which Drake lost two dozen men. The Armada re-formed and once more headed east, but to what destination?

The Isle of Wight

For all the English knew, Medina Sidonia might attempt to land his army on the English coast. At the same time, Parma might try to dash across the Channel from Dunkirk. It was to prevent this that Seymour had been stationed off the coast of Flanders. Evidently,

The English engage the Spanish fleet (in their familiar crescent formation) off the Isle of Wight.

the English did not realize that Justin of Nassau and his sea beggars would be able to prevent Parma's crossing.

Howard reasoned that Medina Sidonia's target might be the Isle of Wight, a lightly defended island about twenty miles long that lies off England's southern coast. Medina Sidonia, indeed, was considering a landing on the Isle of Wight, but not as part of an invasion of England. In the first place, he was running short of food and water. Even more critical, he had received no word from Parma despite having sent numerous messages. Until he knew exactly when and where Parma would meet him, Medina Sidonia did not want to sail to Flanders, where there were no deepwater ports in which he could take shelter. Instead, he might capture the Isle of Wight and use it as a base from which he might replenish his supplies and make final arrangements with Parma.

The morning of August 4 found the Spaniards at the western end of The Solent, the narrow channel between the Isle of Wight and the English coast. This entrance was too narrow for the Armada, and there was no place to land on the seaward shore of the Isle of Wight. Therefore, the Armada would have to sail past the Isle of Wight and then north into the eastern entrance if Medina Sidonia chose to do so. As things turned out, the Spanish admiral did not get a chance to make the choice.

The previous night, Howard had rearranged his fleet, dividing it into four distinct squadrons commanded by himself, Hawkins, Drake, and Frobisher. At dawn, Howard saw that two more ships had drifted away from the Armada and sent Hawkins after them. Since there was no wind, Hawkins had to lower boats and be towed by rowers toward his target. Medina Sidonia sent three galleasses toward Hawkins's squadron. To have more firepower, they towed with them Leiva in *La Rata Encoronada*.

More Trouble for Frobisher

Meanwhile, Frobisher, using a strong eastern water current, tried to edge around the Armada to the north, taking only a few ships with him for support. When a slight breeze began, Frobisher found himself in trouble. His huge *Triumph* was not very maneuverable in light winds, and he was within range of the northern wing of the Armada. Medina Sidonia saw this and led a group of galleons toward him. But, just as it appeared Frobisher would be caught, the light breeze turned to a strong wind and the *Triumph* sped away so fast that the Armada ships, as a Spanish observer wrote, "seemed in comparison with her to be standing still."

The eastern entrance to The Solent now lay open to the Armada. Medina Sidonia had only to give the signal and the entire fleet would swing north into the undefended channel. At that point, however, a furious attack was unleashed against the Ar-

Shipboard Dining

With no way to keep food fresh, the quality of meals on long voyages was usually poor. Since vegetables and fruit would spoil after a short time, ship's crews were subject to disease, especially scurvy (a gum disease) and typhoid fever, sometimes called "ship fever."

At the time of the Armada, the daily food allowance for the common Spanish seaman or soldier was 1½ pounds of biscuit or two pounds of fresh bread, 1⅓ pints of wine or one pint of the stronger Candia wine, and three pints of water (for drinking and washing).

Each Sunday and Thursday, each man received six ounces of bacon and two ounces of rice. Each Monday and Wednesday there was six ounces of cheese and three ounces of dried beans or peas. On Wednesdays, Fridays, and Saturdays, each man got six ounces of fish (tuna, cod, squid, or sardines), 1½ ounces of oil, and a quarter pint of vinegar.

Each English seaman received on Sundays, Tuesdays, and Thursdays a pound of biscuits, a gallon of beer, two pounds of beef, four ounces of cheese, and two ounces of butter. On Wednesdays, Fridays, and Saturdays, the ration was one pound of biscuits, a gallon of beer, a quarter of a stockfish or an eighth of a ling (a fish), four ounces of cheese, and two ounces of butter. The allotment for Mondays was one pound of bacon, one pint of peas, four ounces of cheese, and two ounces of butter.

A major difference in the two fleets was that English ships had galleys, shipboard kitchens where meals for the entire crew were prepared. The Spanish crews were divided into groups of eight or ten men called *camaradas*. Each group drew its rations and took turns preparing its meals in the galley using its own pots and dishes.

mada's southern flank. It was Drake, who again had worked his way to sea and was in position to take advantage of the new wind.

In the face of his charge, the southernmost Spanish ships retreated to the northeast and threatened to break away altogether from the main body of the Armada. Medina Sidonia now had no choice but to sail east to the rescue. Otherwise the English would have accomplished what they had been unable to do all week—break up the Armada's formation.

When Medina Sidonia approached with the main body of the Armada, Drake broke off his attack. By now, however, the Spaniards were east of the point of land known as Sedley Bill and the Ower Banks, with their shallow water and treacherous currents. It would have been difficult, if not impossible, for him to go back around them, against the wind and facing the English fleet, to enter The Solent. The duke had no choice but to head east toward Flanders. Howard had not been able to stop the Armada, but at least he had prevented it from landing on English soil. What awaited both fleets at Flanders, no one knew.

CHAPTER FOUR

The Battle of the Narrow Seas

Would Medina Sidonia successfully hook up with the duke of Parma's (pictured) army to defeat the English?

For five days the Spanish Armada had sailed up the English Channel, hounded all the way by the English. Medina Sidonia was nearing his goal but had no idea what awaited him. Was the duke of Parma's army ready? Where and how would they meet? Howard and the English had questions, too. How could they break up this mighty force, which so far had resisted their best efforts? The answers, for both commanders, would not be long in coming, and they would change the course of history.

Medina Sidonia knew that his fleet could find no deepwater port in Flanders, where Parma awaited him. Instead, on August 5 and 6, he crossed the Channel, dropping anchor off the port of Calais, which, after two hundred years of English rule, had become French in 1558. The English fleet stayed a half-mile behind but did not attack, mainly because it was almost out of shot and powder. After nightfall, Howard received fresh ammunition from the English mainland and also received reinforcements. Lord Henry Seymour had ignored Queen Elizabeth's instruction to patrol the waters off Dunkirk and brought his squadron of about forty-five warships to join Howard. For the first time, the English felt themselves equal in strength to the Armada and ready for an all-out battle.

While the news for Howard was good, the tidings for Medina Sidonia were all bad. He had sent repeated messages to Parma, asking where and when their meeting was to take place. Finally, on the morning of Sunday, August 7, he received an answer. He had hoped Parma would have loaded his troops on barges, ready to sail, but Parma's message, his first to the Armada's commander, was that it would be six days before the Army of Flanders would be ready. Even worse, the duke was told by one of his messengers who had seen Parma and his troops that those six days would be more like fourteen, at the least.

The duke was stunned. His fleet was in a dangerous position because of strong local currents. The sympathetic governor of Calais had provided the Spaniards with food—at high prices— but was afraid to anger the English by supplying Medina Sidonia with powder and shot. The duke wrote to Parma:

> I am anchored here two leagues [about five miles] from Calais with the enemy's fleet on my flank. They can cannonade me whenever they like, and I shall be unable to do them much harm in return. If you give me forty or fifty fly-boats [small warships like the Dutch cromsters] of your fleet, I can, with their help, defend myself here until you are ready to come out.

The Fire Ships

This was wishful thinking. Parma had fewer than twenty such ships and half of those were not seaworthy. As the Armada's commander pondered what to do next, the decision was taken from him.

Howard, Drake, and the other English leaders knew that a critical time had come. They could not allow the Armada simply to sit and wait until a way was devised to link up with Parma. They had to drive the Spaniards from their anchorage and decided that the best way was to send in fire ships.

Fire was the thing most feared among men on wooden sailing ships. The slightest spark on a weathered deck, spar, sail, or rope could set an entire vessel ablaze in minutes. For centuries, one tactic of naval war had been to set empty ships on fire and let them drift or sail into the middle of a fleet at anchor.

During the night, everything valuable was stripped from eight ships, none smaller than ninety tons. Their holds were stuffed with anything that could burn. Masts and rigging were smeared with tar. Guns were loaded so that they would fire on their own when hot enough. Volunteers were picked to sail the ships as close as possible to the Armada before leaping overboard and swimming back to waiting boats.

Shortly after midnight, lookouts high in the rigging of the Armada saw a light from the direction of the English fleet. Gradually, the light grew brighter, then became a glowing line across

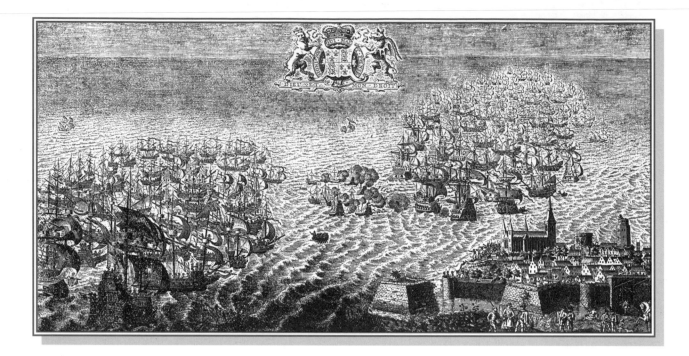

A depiction of the English (left) and Spanish (right) fleets off the shore of Calais (foreground). The English fire ships can be seen in the center, heading toward their Spanish targets.

the water. Eventually, the Spaniards were able to make out eight flaming ships heading directly at them.

Medina Sidonia had been expecting a fire ship attack and had positioned a number of *pataches* to intercept them, latch onto them with grappling hooks, and tow them away from the Armada. The English fire ships, however, were much larger than expected. Even though the *pataches* succeeded in dragging two of the burning ships off course, the rest bore down on the Armada.

The Spaniards had reason to fear these fire ships more than usual. Three years before, when the city of Antwerp was under siege by Dutch and English troops, fire ships had been sent against the city's bridges. Unlike normal fire ships, these had been rigged by an Italian engineer named Giambelli to explode at various times. One such ship, packed with brick, stones, and musket balls, exploded when it hit a bridge crowded with spectators, who had thought it harmless. More than eight hundred Spanish troops were killed by what came to be called a "hell-burner." Since Giambelli was known to be living in England, the Spaniards of the Armada feared that the ships approaching them were floating bombs.

Thus it was that when the fire ships' guns, now white-hot, began to fire and Medina Sidonia gave the signal for his ships to get out of the way, the Spanish captains panicked. Instead of slipping their anchor cables—unfastening them and securing them to a floating buoy so that they could be recovered—most of the captains simply cut their anchor cables and fled in every direction.

The Armada Is Scattered

As it happened, the fire ships did no actual damage, eventually going aground on the beach and burning out. When Medina Sidonia saw that they were past, he returned to the original anchorage and fired a gun as a signal for the rest of the Armada to rejoin him. It couldn't. By now, his ships were spread over several square miles. Many who had cut their cables had no way of anchoring at all. While the fire ships had not damaged a single Spanish vessel, they had accomplished something far more helpful to the English—scattering the Armada.

When dawn came on Monday, August 8, Medina Sidonia saw that he had been joined by no more than half a dozen galleons, including the *San Marcos* with the marquis de Pinafiel, the *San Juan* with Recalde, and the *Santa Ana* with Oquendo. The rest were strung out northeastward toward the sandbanks off the Flemish city of Dunkirk. The duke hurried after them, determined to bring the Armada together once again. Howard immediately ordered the English to attack, and the Battle of Gravelines, named for the Flemish town on the shore nearby, began.

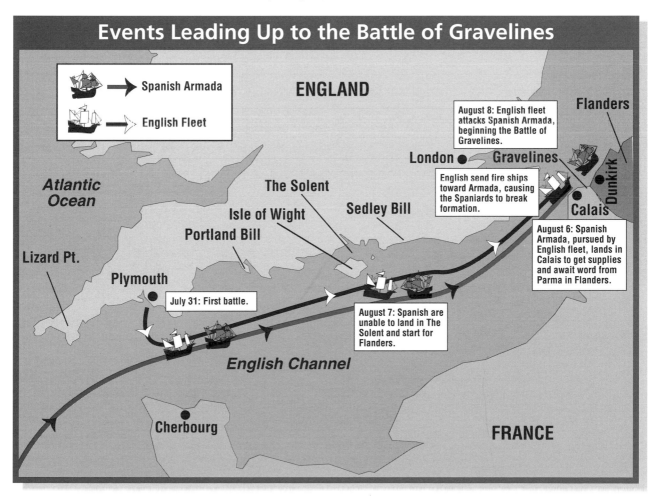

Events Leading Up to the Battle of Gravelines

Spanish Armada

English Fleet

ENGLAND

Atlantic Ocean

Flanders

August 8: English fleet attacks Spanish Armada, beginning the Battle of Gravelines.

London ● Gravelines

English send fire ships toward Armada, causing the Spaniards to break formation.

The Solent

Dunkirk

Isle of Wight

Sedley Bill

Calais

Portland Bill

August 6: Spanish Armada, pursued by English fleet, lands in Calais to get supplies and await word from Parma in Flanders.

Lizard Pt.

Plymouth

July 31: First battle.

August 7: Spanish are unable to land in The Solent and start for Flanders.

English Channel

Cherbourg

FRANCE

The Battle of Gravelines

The most descriptive eyewitness account of the Battle of Gravelines came from Pedro Calderón, a minor officer on board the *San Salvador:*

The enemy opened a heavy artillery fire on our flagship [Medina Sidonia's *San Martín*] at seven o'clock in the morning, which was continued for nine hours. So tremendous was the fire that over 200 [cannon]balls struck the sails and hull of the flagship on the starboard [right] side, killing and wounding many men, disabling and dismounting guns and destroying much rigging. The holes made in the hulls between wind and water [just above the waterline] caused so great a leakage that two divers had as much as they could to stop them with tow [sticky fibers] and lead plates working all day.

The Duke's flagship . . . and the *San Salvador* luffed [sailed] up as close as possible and went to the aid of the [*San Felipe*]. The *San Salvador* engaged an admiral's and a commodore's flagships, her bows, side, and half her poop [rear deck] being exposed for four hours to the enemy's fire, during which she had a larger number of men killed and wounded, and her hull, her sails and rigging were much damaged. She leaked greatly through shot holes, and finally the *Rata Encoronada*, under Don Alonso de Leyva [Leiva], came to her assistance, distinguishing herself greatly. On board the *Rata* there fell Don Pedro de Mendoza and other persons. They had to defend themselves against three flagships, a vice-flagship and ten or twelve other war vessels. This engagement lasted until four o'clock in the afternoon, the *San Juan* and the *San Marcos* suffering very severely. Don Felipe de Cordoba, son of Don Diego, his Majesty's Master of Horse, had his head shot off.

The Duke's flagship lost 40 soldiers, and Sergeant Juan Carrasco, Alonso de Orozco and others. Diego Enriquez, who succeeded to the command of Pedro de Valdes' [captain of the captured *Rosario*] squadron, also fought bravely in this engagement, and his ship suffered to such an extent that every one of his sails were destroyed. Don Pedro Enriquez had a hand shot away in this fight, and the ship's company generally behaved with great gallantry.

The English ships were swifter than the Spanish, and Medina Sidonia, seeing that he would be overtaken, decided to turn and fight, hoping the rest of the Armada would reassemble. Drake's squadron was the first to attack, but his tactics were different than in the Channel. He sailed close to the *San Martín*—though not close enough to be boarded—and fired a broadside into the Spanish flagship. His ships followed close behind, each one blazing away as it passed the Spaniards, who fired back as best they could. This was the first battle of the type that would mark warfare at sea for the next three hundred years. Not until the development of steam-driven, iron battleships with their huge guns would sea battles be fought at long distances.

The English had two reasons for abandoning their strategy of long-range bombardment. First, it had not worked. They had not slowed the advance of the Armada, something they now felt they must do. Second, in the few times there had been close-range fighting over the past week, the Spaniards had been able to do little damage. The English had noticed that, after an initial broadside, the rate of fire from Spanish guns was extremely slow—one shot for every three from English ships. Historians have speculated that the Armada was trying to save shot. Exploration of wrecks of Armada ships have shown, however, that the Spaniards had plenty of shot. Their problems were inefficient gun crews and the awkward design of the guns and their carriages.

Drake Under Fire

This is not to say the Spaniards were incapable of doing any damage. Drake's *Revenge* came under heavy fire. A story goes that Drake's cabin was twice pierced by cannonballs, one of which smashed the bed on which the duke of Northumberland was "lying weary" from the battle. Another account said that the *Revenge* was "pierced above forty times with shot." After firing their initial broadsides, however, the Spaniards could only fire haphazardly while taking a severe battering from the English.

Once Drake's squadron was past the *San Martín*, it headed north to attack some of the scattered Spanish ships before they could come to their admiral's aid. First Frobisher, leading his squadron in the *Triumph*, then Hawkins in the *Victory* came in behind Drake and continued the attack against Medina Sidonia and his handful of galleons.

No full account of the Battle of Gravelines has survived, only a few eyewitness versions of isolated events. Apparently, the Spaniards tried, with some success, to re-form their crescent. Three galleasses joined Medina Sidonia as did Leiva in *La Rata Encoronada*. Sir William Wynter, a captain in Seymour's squadron, wrote later that the Spaniards "went into a proportion of a half moon . . . and there went on each side . . . in the whole to a number of sixteen in a wing." Therefore, the Armada's famous crescent, which had numbered more than one hundred ships in the Channel, could muster only slightly more than thirty at Gravelines.

It was about 10 A.M., three hours into the battle, before Howard joined the rest of his fleet. Shortly after dawn, his attention had been diverted by the galleass *San Lorenzo*, Hugo de Moncada's flagship, which had lost her rudder in the confusion following the fire ship attack. She had tried to row to Calais harbor but had gone aground on a sandbank and was tilted over, seaward guns pointing uselessly at the sky.

Howard could not resist such a prize, and after sending Drake, Frobisher, and Hawkins after Medina Sidonia, he headed for the *San Lorenzo*. He could not get close enough to board because of the shallow water, so he lowered boats with a boarding party. As the English neared, the Spaniards put up a stout defense that ended only when Moncada was killed by a musket shot through the head.

As the remaining Spaniards leaped overboard and swam to shore, the victorious English swarmed over the stricken ship, stripping her of everything of value. Howard would have liked to have taken the entire ship, towing her off the sandbank, but the governor of Calais sent messengers telling the English that since the ship had been wrecked on his doorstep, she was his property. The English argued, even roughing up the French messengers and stealing some of their jewelry. The governor responded by turning the huge guns on his city walls on the English boats and threatening to blow them out of the water. Howard was forced to withdraw and joined the main battle.

Hugo de Moncada (pictured), commander of the San Lorenzo, *was shot in the head while defending his ship during the English attack. (Right) Howard and his sailors then boarded the* San Lorenzo *in order to seize any valuables on the ship.*

The Crescent Is Broken

Meanwhile, as Drake fought to the north of what remained of the Spanish formation, Frobisher and Hawkins attacked the points of the crescent and succeeded in separating enemy ships from the formation and surrounding them. Medina Sidonia was forced to send ships to rescue those under attack, and after about an hour, the Armada's formation fell apart and it became every ship for herself.

On the eastern side of the battle, the Portuguese galleon *San Felipe*, commanded by Don Francisco de Toledo, was separated and surrounded by Seymour's squadron. So close did the English ships come that the Spanish soldiers were able to kill many of their enemy with musket fire. The *San Felipe*, however, had no answer for the English guns, which, according to Spanish eyewitness Pedro Calderón, "kept up a hot artillery fire . . . disabling the rudder, breaking the foremast and killing over 200 men in the galleon."

The *San Felipe*'s plight was noticed by Don Diego Pimentel in the galleon *San Mateo*, which tried to come to the rescue. Instead, she received the same treatment as the *San Felipe*. One English ship sailed so close that a daring Englishman leaped onto the enemy's deck, where, Calderón wrote, "our men cut him to bits instantly."

The *San Felipe* was a floating wreck. Five of her heavy guns had been knocked out of action, pumps had been broken, and rigging and sails were in tatters. Don Francisco shouted at the nearest English ship to come alongside and fight. Instead, wrote Calderón,

> one Englishman, standing in the maintop [the top of the center mast] with his sword and buckler [shield], called out: "Good soldiers that ye are, surrender to the fair terms we offer ye." But the only answer he got was a gunshot, which brought him down in the sight of everyone. . . . The enemy thereupon retired, whilst our men shouted out to them that they were cowards, and with opprobrious [contemptuous] words reproached [rebuked] them for their want [lack] of spirit, calling them Lutheran [Protestant] hens [the equivalent of "chicken"] and daring them to return to the fight.

The smoke of battle now was so thick that Medina Sidonia could not follow the fighting. Climbing high in the rigging of the *San Martín*, he saw the plight of the *San Felipe* and *San Mateo* and sent Recalde with four ships of his squadron to try to hold off the English. At first, they succeeded in throwing a protective ring around the two stricken galleons, but when Howard joined the attack, Recalde was forced to withdraw.

Carnage on the Decks

The English did not linger to try to capture, or even sink, the battered ships. Instead, they moved on to other targets, raking each one with gunfire, shattering masts, tearing sails apart, and leaving decks littered with dead and dying men before seeking another foe. It was not the cannonballs themselves that cut down so many men as much as it was the jagged splinters that flew in all directions when the shot struck wooden decks and railings.

The Armada fought bravely despite severe damage. One of the Spanish survivors remembered seeing "through the portholes an Italian ship [probably the *San Juan de Sicilia*] all full of blood, which yet maintained the fight." Another saw Bertendona's *La Regazona*—blood spilling off her deck, big guns silent—wheeling back to take her place in formation, ready to attack with only the musketeers in the rigging and on the quarterdeck.

The greatest danger to the Armada, however, was not the English ships, but the strong west wind that threatened to pile the entire Spanish fleet onto the Dunkirk sandbanks. There, the Spaniards would face certain death—cannonaded by the English, their ships broken up by the waves, and any survivors snapped up by the Dutch in their cromsters. At about 4 P.M., it seemed as if the Armada had only another hour or so to live before it was driven aground.

Suddenly, however, a blinding rainstorm separated the two fleets. As the English saw to the safety of their own ships, the Armada was able to claw its way northeast, out of range of the English guns and a safer distance from the sandbanks. Given this short time, the Spaniards sought frantically to repair what damage they could. Masts were spliced together. Sails and ropes were mended as much as possible. Naked divers went over the side of ships with patches made of thin sheets of lead and sticky oakum to hold them in place, trying to cover the holes made by English gunfire. Men strained at the pumps, trying to empty the water that had leaked through the shot holes.

When the storm had passed at about 5 P.M., Medina Sidonia could see once more the white sails of the English fleet heading for him. He gave a signal for the Armada to go into its crescent formation

English sailors keep up a rapid fire with muskets and cannon while others care for the wounded.

The Firing of Guns

To load and fire a gun or cannon aboard ship in 1588 involved several steps. Since breech-loading guns—those loaded by swinging open the rear of the gun on hinges—had not been invented, almost everything had to be done from the end of the barrel.

First came the charge of gunpowder. It would have been too dangerous to have barrels of powder on deck, so individual charges were made up below deck and wrapped in canvas packages. This powder cartridge was put into the muzzle, then rammed down into the barrel with a long-handled rammer. On top of the cartridge was the wadding, usually a piece of cloth, followed by the ball and another piece of wadding to hold everything in place.

Once the gun was run out through the port, the gunner filled the vent—a small hole in the breech toward the rear of the gun—with powder. When the gun was on target, the gunner touched a flame to the "touch hole," setting off the powder in the vent, which burned down to the cartridge. The cartridge exploded, firing the ball. After each shot, the gun was swabbed out with a wet sponge on the end of a pole, and the process was repeated.

Although a Dutch engraving of the next century shows a shipboard gun being loaded by a man sitting astride the barrel, experiments showed that the long rammers and sponge poles were too heavy to be handled that way. Large pieces thus had to be brought back in through the gun ports for reloading. This was a great advantage for the English, who had devised rectangular boxes on which guns were laid, unlike the Spanish gun carriages, which were designed for land use and had long "trails" in back.

Reports by men who served in the Armada campaign mention "hauling" guns in to be reloaded. This would seem to mean that the practice of allowing the gun's recoil to bring it back through the port had not been devised. Indeed, some experts have suggested that the reason so many Spanish ships leaked badly after the Battle of Gravelines was that the recoil of their guns against the ropes that held them in place caused the boards of the hull to pull from one another, particularly in the merchant ships that had not been built specifically for war.

and prepare for another attack, but the attack never came. During the lull, Howard had discovered that his ships were woefully low on shot and powder. He knew that the west wind and the condition of the Armada would make it impossible for Medina Sidonia to return to Calais. He decided to stay within sight of the Spaniards and wait to see what the next morning would bring.

Even though the fighting had stopped, the Armada had its hands full. Just before sunset, *La María Juan* signaled that she was sinking. Medina Sidonia came alongside and was able to take only one boatload of men before *La María Juan* went to the bottom with 250 men. It was the first ship on either side actually sunk by enemy gunfire.

The surviving ships of the Armada retreat, "saved by God's mercy," according to Medina Sidonia.

Don Francisco de Toledo thought his *San Felipe* was in danger of sinking, too. He signaled for help to the hulk *Doncella*, which was able to take three hundred men from the *San Felipe*, including Don Francisco. When the *Doncella's* captain said that he thought his own ship was in danger of sinking, Don Francisco demanded to be taken back to the *San Felipe*, vowing that he would rather be drowned aboard his own ship. In the end, the *San Felipe* did not sink but, instead, along with the *San Mateo*, drifted from the Armada during the night and went aground off Dunkirk to become the prey of the Dutch.

The Greatest Danger

When the sun rose on Tuesday, August 9, the Armada was in worse danger than the day before. The wind had shifted to the northwest, and the Spaniards were being blown steadily toward the shore of Zeeland, where more treacherous sandbanks awaited them. They could not anchor, most having left their anchors behind during the fire ship attack at Calais. Behind them were the English, ready to use the last of their powder and shot to pound the Spanish ships once they were helpless on the beach.

Medina Sidonia's flagship, the *San Martín*, drew five fathoms. That is, it needed water at least that deep—about thirty feet—or the keel would scrape the bottom. As the water grew more shallow—six fathoms, then 5½—the duke's staff pleaded with him to take the banner that had been blessed by the pope and escape in a *patache*. Medina Sidonia refused. Instead, he made his confession to a priest and "prepared to die like a Christian soldier."

When disaster was only yards away, the wind hesitated, then shifted to the southwest, filling the tattered sails of the Armada and allowing it to sail to safety. "We were saved by God's mercy," Medina Sidonia later said. Indeed, it seemed as if the Spaniards had experienced a miracle, although not exactly the miracle for which King Philip had hoped.

The English could only watch helplessly as the Armada made its way into the North Sea. They did not have the ammunition for an attack. Medina Sidonia did not know this, but even if he had, his fleet was in no shape to launch its own charge. The wind was against him. Most of his prime fighting ships were severely damaged.

On Tuesday night, the duke called a meeting of his admirals. Some wanted to attempt to fight their way back south, but most realized that this was now impossible. The only option open to the Armada was to return to Spain, not the way they had come, but by sailing in a complete circle around the British Isles, a journey of more than fifteen hundred miles. Reluctantly, Medina Sidonia gave the order. He must have known, given the condition of his fleet, that it would be a terrible ordeal.

Howard could not be sure what the Spaniards would do. He reasoned that they would not come south, but he feared they might attempt to land on the eastern coast of England. After ordering Seymour to return to his patrol of the Channel, Howard led the rest of the fleet north after the Armada. At last, on August 12, Howard gave up the chase off the entrance to the Firth of Forth in Scotland. The English headed south, toward home. The Spaniards headed north, toward what would be a terrible fate.

CHAPTER FIVE

The Breath of God

The English, although they did not realize it at the time, had just achieved one of the most important military triumphs in history at the Battle of Gravelines. The Spaniards, although they did not realize it at the time, were about to face an ordeal far worse than English gunfire.

As the Spanish Armada sailed into the North Sea, away from the duke of Parma and his Army of Flanders, the English were afraid either that the Armada might return or that it would attempt to land in England. They knew they had won a victory but thought it was only temporary. "I will not write unto her Majesty [Queen Elizabeth] until more may be done," Howard wrote to Walsingham. "Their force is wonderful great and strong; and yet we pluck their feathers by little and little."

Drake was also cautious, writing:

> God hath given us so good a day in forcing the enemy so far to leeward [against the wind], as I hope in God the Duke of Parma and the Duke of Sidonia shall not shake hands this few days; and whensoever they shall meet, I believe neither of them will greatly rejoice of this day's service. . . . There must be great care taken to send us munitions and victuals [food] whithersoever the enemy goeth.

Since her admirals did not realize the extent of their victory, it is only natural that Queen Elizabeth did not, either. Ever since the Armada had first been sighted off the Lizard, England had been scrambling to prepare her defense against a landing by Parma.

There was no English army to speak of, only the "trained bands," or local militias consisting mostly of civilians with no experience in war. Nevertheless, Elizabeth's captain-general, the earl of Leicester, managed to gather a force of about ten thousand soldiers at Tilbury in southeastern England. On August 18, the same day that Howard's ships returned, Elizabeth rode among her troops dressed in white velvet and wearing a breastplate of silver. From the back of a white horse, she spoke to her army:

> I am come amongst you as you see, at this time, not for my recreation and disport, but being resolved, in the midst and heat of the battle, to live or die amongst you all, and to lay down for my God and for my kingdom and for my people, my honour and my blood, even in the dust. I know I have the body of a weak and feeble woman, but I have the heart and stomach of a king, and of a king of England, too, and think foul scorn that Parma or Spain, or any prince of Europe should dare to invade the borders of my realm; to which, rather than any dishonour shall grow by me, I myself will take up arms, I myself will be your general, judge, and rewarder of everyone of your virtues in the field.

Queen Elizabeth addresses her troops at Tilbury. The English were still preparing for a land invasion, unaware that the Royal Navy had already defeated the Armada.

No Praise, No Thanks

Queen Elizabeth (above) was unappreciative of her navy's defeat of the Armada, scolding Lord Howard (below) for spending too much money on supplies.

Elizabeth's sailors received precious little reward. In her first letter to Howard, she did not congratulate her Lord Admiral on his victory but instead rebuked him for the great amount of powder and shot he had used and demanded to know what treasure he had brought and what ships he had captured.

The common seamen fared even worse. Elizabeth wanted to disband the fleet immediately so that she would not have to pay the men. The day after her Tilbury speech, however, a report came that Parma would attempt a Channel crossing within the next few days. So, instead of thanking the men who had beaten the Armada, Elizabeth kept them aboard their ships for weeks, ready to sail again, while disease killed far more than had the Spaniards.

Late in August, word finally came that Parma had unloaded his boats and sent his soldiers inland. About the same time an English sea captain reported having sighted the Armada west of the Orkney Islands far to the north of Scotland. Since the danger was apparently over, Elizabeth disbanded the fleet, leaving thousands of men sick, starving, and with only a promise of payment. Howard spent practically all his own money on food and shelter for his former sailors, even as bonfires were lit throughout the country to celebrate the victory they had won. Indeed, England had the idea that the Armada had been defeated, not by her fleet, but by divine intervention. A medallion was made to commemorate the occasion reading, in Latin, "He [God] breathed and they were scattered."

If at first the English had little idea of what had happened at Gravelines, the rest of Europe had even less. It was known that the Armada had reached the English Channel and that there had been fighting there, but that was all. In Paris, King Philip's ambassador to France, Don Bernadino de Mendoza, heard rumors that the Spaniards had landed in England and other rumors that the Spaniards had been defeated. Then word came from the French port of Le Havre that some fishermen had witnessed a great battle in which fifteen English galleons were sunk.

Mendoza accepted the story and wrote to King Philip, proclaiming a great victory, which he was confident would be verified at any time. He piled a huge bonfire in the courtyard of his embassy, ready to be lit when confirmation of the victory came. He went to the French royal court at Chartres on August 12, encouraging King Henri III to order a great service in the cathedral to celebrate the Catholic triumph.

An Unwelcome Letter

Henri listened to Mendoza in silence and then said, "Your news, if it were certain, would be most welcome. But we, too, have news from Calais which you may wish to see." Mendoza was handed a letter from the governor of Calais, who reported that the Armada had fled into the North Sea after a fire ship attack with the English in pursuit. Stunned, Mendoza could only reply, "Obviously, our reports differ." He returned to Paris, and his bonfire remained unlit.

For the next two weeks, rumors continued to fly: The *Ark Royal* had been sunk and Howard captured; Drake had had his leg shot off; Drake had been captured while trying to board the *San Martín*; Medina Sidonia had landed in Scotland and was about to return to Flanders; the Catholics in England had risen in rebellion against Elizabeth, who had to flee for her life.

The Spanish ambassador in Rome saw Pope Sixtus V and asked him not only to hold a special victory service, but also to pay the first installment of the promised million ducats. The pope hesitated. He had received other reports, he told the Spanish ambassador. Perhaps it would be better to wait. He would not have to wait long.

On August 17, the pope received a report from his representative in France, the bishop of Brescia. It probably had been given to the bishop by Sir Edward Stafford, English ambassador to France, and was a summary of Howard's report to Elizabeth's council. At about the same time, the report was published in Paris, doubtless by Stafford, in an effort to publicize the English victory.

The faith of Spain in its Armada was shaken but not broken. The report was an English lie, claimed Mendoza. The Armada had landed in Scotland to take on fresh supplies, he said, and even then was heading south toward Parma. Then other reports began to reach Europe, terrible reports the Spaniards did not want to believe. These reports were not from England, but from Ireland.

On August 21, the Armada—112 ships of the 130 that had sailed from Lisbon—had sailed between the Orkney and Shetland Islands into the North Atlantic. Medina Sidonia dispatched one of his officers, Balthasar de Zúñiga, in a speedy *patache* to take news of what had happened to King Philip. Although food and water supplies were low and about three thousand men were sick or wounded, the duke said he hoped to bring most of his fleet safely back to Spain. No sooner had Zúñiga departed than disaster struck.

Acting on rumors that the Armada had successfully defeated the Royal Navy, a Spanish ambassador in Rome unsuccessfully tried to convince Pope Sixtus V (pictured) to give Spain promised money for the victory.

The English Strategy

Lord Howard, Sir Francis Drake, and the rest of the English admirals knew from the start that they could not hope to win a battle with the Spanish Armada fought the way naval battles had been fought throughout history—pulling alongside an enemy and overwhelming him with soldiers. After the first day's fighting, Howard wrote, "We durst [dared] not put among them, their fleet being so strong."

These tactics did not sit well with everyone in the English fleet. Henry White, captain of the *Talbot*, which later became one of the fire ships used at Calais, was unhappy at what he considered an unmanly, if not cowardly, way of doing battle. He wrote:

> The majesty of the enemy's fleet, the good order they held, and the private consideration of our own wants did cause, in mine opinion, our first onset to be more coldly done than became the value of our nation and the credit of the English navy.

White's opinion was shared by Queen Elizabeth and many at her court, who after the defeat of the Armada criticized Howard, Sir Francis Drake, and all the rest for not having boarded numerous Spanish ships and bringing them back as prizes. Such lack of understanding caused Sir Walter Raleigh, one of Elizabeth's courtiers and a seaman himself, to write twenty years later in his *History of the World*:

> He that will happily perform a fight at sea must believe that there is more belonging to a good man of war upon the waters than great daring, and must know there is a great deal of difference between fighting loose and grappling. To clap ships together without consideration belongs rather to a madman than to a ship of war; for by such an ignorant bravery was Peter Strozzi lost at the Azores when he fought against the Marquis of Santa Cruz. In like sort had the Lord Charles Howard, Admiral of England, been lost in the year 1588 if he had not been better advised than a great many malignant fools were who found fault with his behavior.

The Fateful Storm

On the night of August 22, a powerful storm blew in on a southwest wind. The Spanish ships, battered and lacking full crews, had no choice but to run before the wind, that is to turn in the direction of the wind and let it blow them where it might. The storm blew for almost two weeks. When it finally ended, Medina Sidonia found himself far back to the east. Only about sixty ships were still with him. The rest had scattered.

The ships that found themselves apart from the main body of the Armada were in terrible trouble. Low on food, most of their crews ill, they had no chance of reaching Spain without first landing somewhere. Many were in danger of sinking and had to reach land—any land—as soon as possible.

El Gran Grifón, the flagship of the Spanish hulks, tried to reach the Atlantic once more but had to run ashore at Fair Isle, a small island midway between the Orkneys and Shetlands. The ship ran aground on a beach, but fortunately its foremast lay against the side of a cliff. Most of the crew were able to climb the mast to safety, but almost nothing could be saved from the ship.

A few families lived on Fair Isle, and, to their credit, the Spaniards left them alone. There was plenty of fish and seabirds, but fifty of *El Gran Grifón*'s crew died before contact could be made with the Shetlands. Eventually, the survivors were taken to Scotland as prisoners and after months of negotiations, were allowed to return to Spain. They were lucky. Scotland was technically a neutral country, where the shipwrecked Spaniards had a reasonable chance of survival. Most were not so fortunate and were driven ashore in Ireland.

Medina Sidonia had specifically told his ships to avoid Ireland "for fear of the harm that may happen unto you upon that coast." Ireland was one of the wildest and most remote parts of Europe. Although they were Catholics, the Irish were considered savages by other Europeans, and the Spaniards feared they would receive a harsh welcome.

Furthermore, Ireland was ruled by England, although English control was strong only on the east coast around Dublin. Sir William Fitzwilliam, Elizabeth's Lord Deputy in Ireland, had only 750 troops with which to try to keep the peace. He had been alerted to be on the lookout for Spanish ships, since an invasion of Ireland by the Armada was still considered possible. Since he did not have enough men to guard large numbers of prisoners, Fitzwilliam sent out orders to his troops to "apprehend and execute all Spaniards found, of what quality soever."

The Irish Ordeal

One of the first Spanish ships in Ireland was *La Trinidad Valencera*, which was grounded on a reef at the west end of Kinnagoe Bay. The captain, Don Alonso de Luzón, and four men went ashore in a small boat to seek help. When they landed, about twenty "savage people" robbed them of "money, gold buttons, rapiers [swords] and apparel to the value of 7,300 ducats."

Luzón finally succeeded in getting most of his crew ashore and headed for the west coast, hoping to catch a ship for Spain. They had gone only twenty miles, however, when they reached a castle belonging to an Irish bishop. The bishop promised to help the Spaniards but then betrayed them to local English troops. Caught in a trap, Luzón surrendered. The English and their Irish allies promptly took the common seamen and soldiers into a nearby field and slaughtered them. Officers, for whom a ransom might be paid, were marched a hundred miles to the city of Drogheda, many dying along the way. Only Luzón and a few others ever saw Spain again.

It was the same up and down the western coast of Ireland. A *patache* with twenty-four men aboard struggled into the Bay of Tralee. The men were taken to the castle of the local English lord, Sir Edward Denny, and after a brief questioning, were executed. The 736-ton *San Esteban* was wrecked just off the coast at Doonberg in County Clare. More than three hundred men were drowned. Another ship was wrecked on nearby Mutton Island. Only four members of the crew reached shore alive, and these men were publicly hanged by the local sheriff.

A terrible storm on September 21 forced several ships, including Recalde's *San Juan de Portugal*, to seek shelter in Blasket Sound at the southwest tip of Ireland. The Spaniards made what repairs they could but were prevented by English patrols from going ashore for food. One captured Spaniard told the English that

> out of the ship there died 4 or 5 every day of hunger and thirst, and yet this ship was one of the best furnished for victuals. . . . There are 80 soldiers and 20 of the mariners sick, and do lie down and die daily, and the rest . . . are very weak, and the Captain very sad and weak. There is left in this flagship . . . no water but what they brought out of Spain, which stinketh marvellously, and the flesh meat they cannot eat. . . . It is a common bruit [saying] among the soldiers that if they may get home again, they will not meddle with the English any more.

The Armada's bad luck continued after its defeat by the English. Here, storms off the coast of Ireland severely batter what remains of the Armada.

Eventually, the *San Juan* and one other ship were able to leave Blasket Sound and reach Spain.

The Savage Irish

Most Spaniards in 1588 knew more about America than they did about Ireland. Ireland was considered backward and uncivilized, and its people were called savages, even though, like the Spaniards, they were Catholics.

Many of the Armada's sailors and soldiers, stumbling onto Irish beaches from their wrecked ships, were robbed of everything of value by the Irish. They seldom were murdered, although the legend grew up later that thousands were killed as they came ashore.

Not all the Irish were unfriendly to the Spaniards. Many Armada survivors were taken in, clothed, and fed by the natives. Francisco de Cuellár, a survivor of *La Lavia*, lived in an Irish village for three months and left this description:

> It is the custom of these savages to live like wild beasts in the mountains. They live in huts made of straw; they eat only once a day and that at nightfall, their usual food being oaten bread and butter. . . . The men dress in tight hose and short coats of coarse goat's hair; over this they wear a blanket, and their hair falls low over their eyes. . . . Their great desire is to be thieves and plunder one another, so that hardly a day passes without a call to arms among them; for as soon as the men of one village discover that there are cattle or anything else in another village they come armed by night and attack and kill each other. . . . Most of the women are very beautiful but poorly dressed; they wear nothing but a smock covered with a blanket, and a linen kerchief folded tightly round their heads and fastened in front. . . . These savages liked us Spaniards well . . . indeed if they had not taken as much care of us as they did of themselves not one of us would be alive.

Another Armada legend is that many of the ships' survivors found homes in Ireland, and that, even now, people along the western coast tend to have Latin features. The truth is that while some members of the Armada may, indeed, have remained in Ireland and found wives there, it would hardly amount to enough to change ethnic characteristics that had been developing for thousands of years.

Cuellár's Story

The most detailed eyewitness report of the Irish ordeal was by Francisco de Cuellár, who had been captain of the galleon *San Pedro* but who had disobeyed one of Medina Sidonia's orders and been placed under arrest aboard *La Lavia*. The September 21 storm forced *La Lavia* and two other ships to seek shelter in Donegal Bay on the northwestern coast. While they waited for a favorable wind, a second storm struck. With most of their anchors having been left in the waters off Calais, the ships were driven ashore and pounded to pieces by the surf. More than eleven hundred men were drowned.

About three hundred men jumped overboard and were able to make it to the shore. Cuellár, who could not swim and remained on the ship, later wrote that the beach was

> full of enemies [Irish] who were going about skipping and dancing with joy at our misfortune. Whenever any of our men reached land, two hundred savages and other enemies rushed upon them and stripped them of everything they wore, leaving them stark naked, and without any pity beat them and ill used them.

La Lavia's captain and a few high-ranking officers climbed aboard a closed boat, taking more than sixteen thousand ducats in gold and jewels with them. After they shut the hatch, however, other sailors swarmed aboard the frail craft, which capsized and sank. When it washed ashore, it was broken open by the Irish, who gleefully stripped the corpses of their valuables and left them unburied on the sand.

Cuellár finally reached the beach, almost naked, and managed to crawl to some brush along with a companion. Two Irishmen discovered them there but took pity and covered them with grass and foliage. When Cuellár awoke the next morning, his companion was dead "on the field with more than 600 other bodies which the sea had cast up. The crows and the wolves fed upon them and there was nobody to bury any of them." A few Irishmen moved among the bodies, looking for loot, clubbing to the ground any Spaniard who tried to rise.

For centuries, the popular belief was that most of the Spaniards who died in the Irish shipwrecks were killed by the wild Irish as they came ashore. While it is true that many survivors were robbed by the natives, the deaths came mostly as a result of drowning or at the hands of English troops.

The Greatest Tragedy

The greatest tragedy of all in Spanish eyes was the fate of *La Rata Encoronada*, upon which had sailed young men from most of Spain's noble houses, all eager to serve under the dashing Leiva. The ship had been unable to keep up with Medina Sidonia and the main body of the Armada and took shelter in Blacksod Bay, high on Ireland's western shore, to make repairs. The anchor failed to hold in the sandy bottom, however, and the ship was grounded on a sandbar.

Leiva managed to get all his crew ashore and then burned the ship, damaged beyond repair. A few miles away, they discovered another Spanish ship, the *Duquesa Santa Ana*. Since there were far too many men—about eight hundred—to attempt to sail to Spain, Leiva decided to try to sail north to the west coast of Scotland. The *Duquesa* had made about one hundred miles

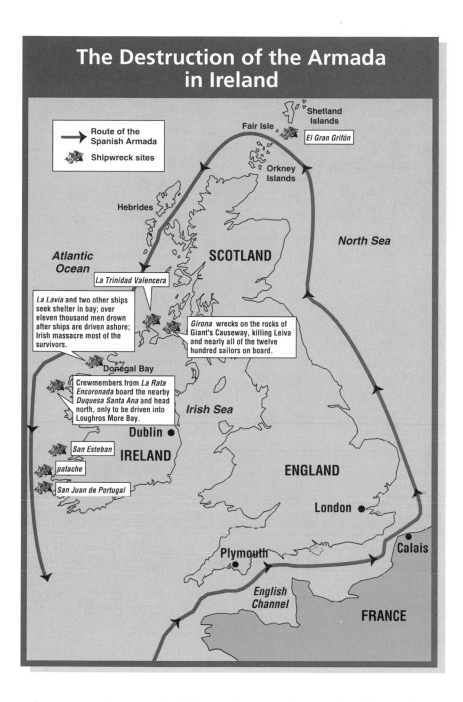

The Destruction of the Armada in Ireland

Legend:
→ Route of the Spanish Armada
Shipwreck sites

Labels on map:

Shetland Islands
El Gran Grifón
Fair Isle
Orkney Islands
Hebrides
North Sea
SCOTLAND
Atlantic Ocean
La Trinidad Valencera

La Lavia and two other ships seek shelter in bay; over eleven thousand men drown after ships are driven ashore; Irish massacre most of the survivors.

Girona wrecks on the rocks of Giant's Causeway, killing Leiva and nearly all of the twelve hundred sailors on board.

Donegal Bay

Crewmembers from *La Rata Encoronada* board the nearby *Duquesa Santa Ana* and head north, only to be driven into Loughros More Bay.

Irish Sea
Dublin
San Esteban
IRELAND
patache
San Juan de Portugal
ENGLAND
London
Plymouth
Calais
English Channel
FRANCE

when a northwest wind drove it onto the rocks of Loughros More Bay.

Leiva suffered a leg injury, and most of his crew survived. They stayed near the bay eight days, helped by friendly Irishmen, until word came that the galleass *Girona* was just south of them at Donegal Bay. After spending two weeks making repairs, Leiva set sail again, this time with twelve hundred men aboard. The *Girona* made her way slowly around the northern coast of Ireland, avoiding most of the dangers. But when it was only about forty miles from Scotland, a sudden storm carried away the rudder and the ship piled up on the rocks known as the Giant's Causeway. Only nine men were saved. King Philip was supposed to have said later that the loss of Leiva meant more to him than the loss of all his ships.

For six weeks after the Battle of Gravelines, Spain held its breath, hoping against hope that the rumors of defeat were not true. Then, on September 24, Balthasar de Zúñiga, after a month of battling the same storms that scattered the Armada, appeared at the Spanish court. He had with him letters from Medina Sidonia pleading for help to be ready when the Armada reached Spain.

Zúñiga was too late. Three days earlier and two months to the day since the Invincible Armada had sailed from Corunna, Medina Sidonia arrived with eight shattered galleons at the port of Santander. About the same time, Don Diego Flores de Valdés arrived at Laredo with twenty-two ships, and Oquendo brought five more into ports along the Bay of Biscay.

Philip is reported to have taken the news of the Armada's defeat calmly, saying, "I sent my fleet against men, not against the wind and the waves." According to other accounts, however, the king was beside himself with grief. His private secretary wrote that "His Majesty has felt it more than you would believe possible. . . . I do not know how he could bear such a blow."

The Armada Limps Home

It would be another month before the full extent of the defeat of the Spanish Armada would be known. Battered ships continued to straggle in one by one. The *San Juan de Portugal*, with Recalde too ill to get out of his bunk, limped into port on October 14, one of the last to arrive. Of the 130 ships that had sailed from Lisbon in May, only about 60 had made it home, and many of those were so damaged that they would never go to sea again. Between fifteen and twenty thousand men died, half in battle or by drowning and half from disease, many of them after they had reached Spain.

Among the dead were Recalde and Oquendo. Recalde had been so grief-stricken and bitter upon his return that he refused to see family members and friends. Instead, he asked to be carried to a monastery, where he died nine days later.

Shortly after reaching port, Medina Sidonia, so ill and weak that he sometimes lacked the strength to sign his name, wrote to King Philip:

> I am unable to describe to Your Majesty the misfortunes and miseries that have befallen us, because they are the worst that have been known on any voyage; and some of the ships that put into this port have spent the last fourteen days without a single drop of water.

Miguel de Oquendo was one of the many Spanish sailors who died during the ill-fated expedition.

The Bitterness of Defeat

There are several versions of how King Philip of Spain reacted to the news that his "Most Happy" Armada had met with disaster. The most widespread story is that he took the news calmly, saying he had sent his ships against men, not against wind and waves. When Medina Sidonia's messenger Balthasar de Zúñiga told Philip of the defeat, the king is supposed to have said,

> I give thanks to God by whose hand I have been so endowed that I can put to sea another fleet as great as this we have lost whenever I choose. It does not matter if a stream is sometimes choked, as long as the source flows freely.

Other accounts, however, show that Philip was bitterly disappointed and wanted revenge on the English. An English spy, Anthony Copley, wrote:

> When news of the disgrace of the King's late Armada was brought unto him, being at Mass at that very time in his Chapel, he sware (after Mass was done) a great Oath, that he would waste and consume his Crown, even to the value of a [last] Candlestick (which he pointed to standing upon the Altar) but either he would utterly ruin her Majesty [Queen Elizabeth] and England, or else himself and all Spain become Tributary [subject] to her. Whereby it was most evident that his Desire for Revenge was extreme and implacable [steadfast] towards England.

As it became apparent in October of 1588 that about half the ships and men of the Armada were lost, Philip's anger gave way to grief. When Juan Martínez de Recalde, one of the last of the Armada's captains to reach Spain, sent his report to Philip, the king wrote that he "read it all, although I would rather not have done, because it hurts so much."

By November, the king was suffering a personal agony of doubt, wondering if God had abandoned him. He wrote to his personal chaplain:

> I promise you that unless some remedy is found . . . very soon we shall find ourselves in such a state that we shall wish that we had never been born. . . . And if God does not send us a miracle . . . I hope to die and go to Him before all this happens—which is what I pray for, so as not to see so much ill fortune and disgrace.

The duke took full responsibility for the disaster, reminding Philip that he had not sought to command the Armada and, indeed, had tried to refuse the appointment. He begged to be allowed to return home.

Philip granted his request, and in mid-October a horse-drawn litter, its curtains tightly drawn, attended by only a few servants, made its way slowly south to San Lúcar. No visits were paid along the way to the houses of noblemen, most of whom were in mourning for lost sons. Medina Sidonia lived to serve Spain another twenty-two years, but many who knew him said he was never the same again.

Queen Elizabeth is dressed in the elaborate garb she wore to St. Paul's Cathedral for the thanksgiving service held to celebrate the defeat of the Armada.

In London, on November 24, a great thanksgiving service was held in St. Paul's Cathedral. Queen Elizabeth was carried there in a chariot drawn by two white horses. Behind her came her latest favorite, the earl of Essex, and behind him all the queen's ladies of honor and the highest nobles in the kingdom, including Howard. Somewhat farther back were her other admirals. On the altar were placed the banners captured from Spanish ships.

During the service, a poem written by the queen was sung. It bestowed the credit for England's greatest victory squarely on God, who

> made the winds and waters rise
> To scatter all mine enemies.
> This Joseph's lord and Israel's god,
> The fiery pillar and day's cloud,
> That saved his saints from wicked men
> And drenched the honour of the proud,
> And hath preserved in tender love
> The spirit of his Turtle Dove.

There was not a word about her fleet or the men who sailed in her name.

EPILOGUE

The Dawn of the British Empire

The defeat of the Spanish Armada was not the end of the war between England and Spain. An English counterattack against Portugal in 1589 was a disaster and ruined Drake's reputation. Philip was determined to gain revenge and sent fleets against England in 1596 and 1597, but both were blown back to Spain by contrary winds. Why, then, has the English victory in 1588 been called one of the world's most decisive battles?

King Henri III of France used the opportunity of Spain's defeat to murder his cousin the duke of Guise.

The most immediate benefactors of the Armada's defeat were the Dutch. King Henri III of France, made bold by the Spanish defeat, sought to rid himself of his cousin, the powerful duke of Guise, who was backed by Spain. On December 23, 1588, he had the duke murdered. In the civil war that followed, the duke of Parma was forced to commit much of his army to helping Spain's allies in France. He never had a chance to reconquer the northern provinces of the Netherlands. He was eventually recalled to Spain and died there in disgrace in 1592.

The Dutch continued their war against Spain and finally, led by Justin of Nassau and his brother Maurice, were able to expel the Spaniards in 1595 and establish an independent republic. Meanwhile, Henri III died and was succeeded by his cousin Henry of Navarre who, as King Henri IV, was able to shake off Spanish influence and extend religious toleration to the French Protestants.

The defeat of the Armada thus broke Spain's iron grip on most of Europe. Philip still was the most powerful ruler in the world, but he was no longer seen as all-powerful.

Within months of the Battle of Gravelines, people not only in England, but also in France, the Netherlands, Italy, and Germany were laughing over the fate of the "invincible" Armada. The year 1588 marked the height of Spain's reputation and began her long, slow descent as a world power. Regiomontanus's forecast of the altering of kingdoms and empires had, in one sense, come true.

And what about England? What would have happened had Medina Sidonia and Parma managed to join forces and invade Elizabeth's kingdom? Certainly, there was no force capable of withstanding such an assault. Elizabeth, if she were not removed from the throne completely, would have had to submit to Philip's demands. Roman Catholicism might have once again become the official religion of England, and since Protestant sentiment was so strong, a bloody civil war would probably have taken place.

The Importance to Religion

Queen Elizabeth is depicted with the Spanish Armada in the background. The defeat of the Armada ensured Protestantism's continuance in England.

It is not too extreme to say that the defeat of the Armada saved Protestantism altogether. If Philip could have made England and the Netherlands Catholic and prevented religious toleration in France, he might have then turned against the Protestant princes of Germany. As historian Garrett Mattingly writes:

[The Armada's defeat] guaranteed that religious unity was not to be forced on the heirs of medieval Christendom. . . . The pattern of territorial, ultimately "national" states was beginning to emerge, and after 1588 each major state was not only to be free, but increasingly to feel free, to develop its own individual potentialities without conforming to any externally imposed system of beliefs.

Fully as important to the world's future, perhaps, was the feeling of national pride that swept England after the Armada's defeat. This spirit led to a burst of creativity in science, literature, and drama known now as the Elizabethan era. Heroes of centuries past became national heroes once more in the plays of William Shakespeare and Christopher Marlowe.

The island nation, freed from the threat of invasion, was ready to take its place as a world power. Its navy grew, challenging Spain's for supremacy of the seas. It was no longer content to raid other countries' possessions in the New World, but began its own program of colonization. This colonization would eventually make England, later Great Britain, the world's most powerful nation. The spirit that arose from the defeat of the Spanish Armada would be carried around the world—not only to America, but to Africa, India, and Australia—to what would become a dominion even larger than that of Philip of Spain—the British Empire.

William Shakespeare wrote his plays during the era of national pride and security that followed the defeat of the Armada.

For Further Reading

David Anderson, *The Spanish Armada*. New York: The Hampstead Press, 1988. Short, easily read book for young grades but packs in loads of good information, much of it not found in other books for this level. Plenty of maps, illustrations, and photographs make this a highly recommended book.

Walter Buehr, *The Spanish Armada*. New York: G. P. Putnam's Sons, 1962. Short, simple account of the origin and fate of the Armada. Pen-and-ink illustrations throughout, and the glossary at the end is helpful.

Helen Hanff, *Queen of England: The Story of Elizabeth*. Garden City, NY: Doubleday & Company, 1969. Very simply written biography for young readers. No index or bibliography and few illustrations.

Roger Hart, *Battle of the Spanish Armada*. London: Wayland Publishers, 1973. Highly detailed yet very readable account of the background, battle, and aftermath of the Spanish Armada. Lavishly illustrated with good use of maps.

Will Holwood, *Sir Francis Drake*. Chicago: Childrens Press, 1958. This biography of Drake begins with his service under John Hawkins and tells little of his earlier life. Good account of Drake's voyages in the 1570s as well as the defeat of the Spanish Armada.

Richard Humble, *Ships, Sailors, and the Sea*. New York: Franklin Watts, 1991. Good introduction to the principles of navigation and the history of ships. Good illustrations and maps by David Salariya.

Edith Thacher Hurd, *The Golden Hind*. New York: Thomas Y. Crowell Company, 1960. An exciting story, geared to very young readers, about Francis Drake's round-the-world voyage in 1578.

Frank Knight, *Stories of Famous Ships*. Philadelphia: The Westminister Press, 1966. Short histories of famous ships includes chapters on the *Golden Hind,* in which Drake sailed around the world, and the *Revenge*—Drake's ship during the Armada campaign.

Jean Lee Latham, *Drake: The Man They Called a Pirate*. New York: Harper & Row Publishers, 1960. Fairly complete account of Drake's life and adventures. Somewhat fictionalized to make it a more readable story.

David Macaulay, *Ship*. Boston: Houghton Mifflin Company, 1993. Fictional account of the archaeological exploration of a sunken ship, followed by an account of how the ship was made. Although this particular ship, a Spanish caravel, was an older type and much smaller than most of those in the Armada, the illustrations are very instructive in how ships were constructed.

Diane Stanley and Peter Vennema, *Good Queen Bess: The Story of Elizabeth I of England*. New York: Four Winds Press, 1990. A good, simply written biography with excellent color illustrations by Diane Stanley.

Ralph T. Ward, *Ships Through History*. Indianapolis, IN: Bobbs-Merrill, 1973. Comprehensive history of sailing ships, including a very good chapter on the galleon. Very well illustrated and contains a glossary of terms.

Betka Zamoyska, *Queen Elizabeth I*. New York: McGraw-Hill Book Company, 1981. Very complete biography on a junior high school level. Includes genealogical chart, chronology, index, and bibliography.

Works Consulted

Winston Graham, *The Spanish Armadas.* As the title indicates, this book covers not only the campaign of 1588, but King Philip of Spain's subsequent attacks on England, some of which barely could be called Armadas. Well illustrated, but more maps would have been helpful.

Michael Lewis, *The Spanish Armada.* New York: Thomas Y. Crowell Company, 1960. Some of the author's conclusions about the types of guns in the Spanish and English fleets have since been cast into doubt by other historians, but his descriptions of the battles themselves are among the best.

Colin Martin and Geoffrey Parker, *The Spanish Armada.* New York: W. W. Norton & Company, 1988. One of the most complete stories of the Armada from its inception through its defeat. Includes lists of ships and their captains, detailed descriptions of ships and guns, and plenty of maps and photographs.

Garrett Mattingly, *The Armada.* Boston: Houghton Mifflin Company, 1959. Highly entertaining account, not only of the defeat of the Armada, but also of all the political intrigue in Europe that led up to the events of 1588. Especially good picture of the struggles in France but short on maps and photographs.

Peter Padfield, *Armada.* Annapolis, MD: Naval Institute Press, 1988. Probably the best book on the Armada from a technical standpoint, but may be too technical for readers not familiar with sailing and nautical terms. Wonderful color photographs.

George M. Trevelyan, *History of England: Volume II, The Tudor and Stuart Era.* Garden City, NY: Doubleday and Company, 1953. Paperback reprint of original 1926 work by one of Britain's most renowned historians. The section on the Armada is short but contains an excellent discussion of the consequences of the battle.

Index

Picture Credits

Cover photo: Peter Newark's Military Pictures

The Bettmann Archive, 52

Corbis-Bettmann, 15 (bottom), 77

Culver Pictures, Inc., 21 (top), 62

Hulton Deutsch Collection Limited/Woodfin Camp & Associates, Inc., 9, 21 (bottom), 22 (both), 27

Library of Congress, 10, 12 (both), 13, 15 (top), 17, 19 (top and bottom), 24, 31, 38, 43, 44 (top), 46, 49, 50, 55, 57, 68 (top), 76 (top), 84, 86

North Wind Picture Archives, 8, 14, 25 (bottom), 29 (bottom), 72, 76 (bottom), 89

Peter Newark's Historical Pictures, 29 (top), 33, 34, 36, 42, 44 (bottom), 48, 54 (both), 58, 64, 68 (bottom), 70, 75, 80, 88

Peter Newark's Western Americana, 59

Stock Montage, Inc., 16, 19 (middle), 23, 41, 51, 87

About the Author

William W. Lace is a native of Fort Worth, Texas. He holds a bachelor's degree from Texas Christian University, a master's from East Texas State University, and a doctorate from the University of North Texas. After working for newspapers in Baytown, Texas, and Forth Worth, he joined the University of Texas at Arlington as sports information director and later became the director of the news service. He is now vice chancellor of public affairs for the Tarrant County Junior College District in Fort Worth. He and his wife, Laura, live in Arlington and have two children. Lace has written several books for Lucent, including a biography of artist Michelangelo and a history of the Hundred Years' War.